KU-397-978

Contents

A PENGUIN SPECIAL S211

Britain in the Sixties: Housing

STANLEY ALDERSON

Britain in the Sixties: Housing

STANLEY ALDERSON

Penguin Books

Penguin Books Ltd, Harmondsworth, Middlesex
U.S.A.: Penguin Books Inc., 3300 Clipper Mill Road, Baltimore 11, Md
AUSTRALIA: Penguin Books Pty Ltd, 762 Whitehorse Road, Mitcham,
Victoria

First published 1962

Made and printed in Great Britain
by Cox & Wyman Ltd, London, Fakenham, and Reading
Set in Monotype Baskerville

What I want people to do is look beyond the façade of Euston Arch and see the slums of St Pancras. When they do that, something's bound to happen.

Eric Lyons in the *Daily Herald*

On a warm summer evening the sewer gas rises in low-lying Chelsea and creeps along the little streets of workmen's cottages, each of which cost its lucky owner £10,000.

Angus McGill in the *Listener*

Preface

IN the second half of the twentieth century we have reduced able-bodied, fully employed people to homelessness; we never managed this before we decided that housing should be regarded as a social service. In the second half of the twentieth century a man made nearly £3 million profit in seven years from an investment in land of £35,000; no one did quite so well as this before we adopted planning powers. In the second half of the twentieth century the man who gets the greatest State aid with his housing is the owner-occupier millionaire; this was not so in the days of privilege, before we promulgated the Welfare State.

Market research can now predict the demand for new products within a few per cent; and we have a slum-clearance programme based on figures that show Welwyn Garden City with the same proportion of unfit houses as Stoke Newington, Cheltenham with the same proportion as Swindon, Carshalton with the same proportion as St Pancras. The first serious effort to see that the most money goes to the areas in the greatest need has been taken in the 1961 Housing Act; and the Act works in such a way that Bournemouth qualifies for a higher subsidy than Liverpool. The Government has deliberately reduced the building of council houses in the belief that, except in special cases, private enterprise can do the job better; and virtually no private housing is being built for rent.

We have houses still being lived in which were condemned during – and by the not unduly rigorous standards of – the thirties. We shall very soon be too late to pull down many of the slums for they will actually have fallen down. The Pelican edition of *The Affluent Society* has a champagne cork on its cover. It is hideously apt. The typical British worker can get champagne if he wants it, but he cannot get decent housing. He can just about afford to meet the cost of housing less land. But there is hardly any decent rented housing available; he has difficulty in getting a mortgage; and he will in any case soon have to give up all hope of meeting the cost of land.

None of this was inevitable: none of it is now irremediable. We have the productive resources for more housing and we have the demand for it. Adequate housing is not like higher education or dental services. People do not need to be talked into it. In desperation, as the squatters showed, they will even go out and grab it. By comparison with the provision of higher education and dental services, the provision of adequate housing is child's play. Given the chance, millions of people will actually pay for it. And it does not need much administrative wit to devise a means of withdrawing the subsidies paid to millionaires and distributing them among uncontrolled private tenants who are too poor to afford the rents of council houses even when they are available.

In the near future, discontent must force a change of policy; and it is rare for this point to be reached in the progress of the social services. Free education, free dental and medical services, family allowances, and the rest – all were introduced from above in advance of any widespread agitation. Housing could not have reached its present crisis had the facts not escaped the majority of politicians and socially responsible intellectuals whose reactions to social waste and abuse effectively initiate most reforms.

There has been no comprehensive public inquiry into housing in this country since the Report of the Royal Commission on the Housing of the Working Classes in 1885. The measure of the need for another Royal Commission now is that it would find itself examining many of the same houses as the last one. The only reason there can be for not holding a public inquiry into housing is fear of what it would disclose. At present the Government can gain kudos from voters in Mayfair for its alleged slum-clearance programme. An inquiry would reveal that slums are being created faster than they are being cleared, and that the official definition of a non-slum does not in any case aspire to the lowest depth of civilized living.

So long as we were patching up the bombed houses and requisitioning the unbombed, and so long as we were building new houses as fast as we could, an inquiry into general housing conditions could reasonably be postponed. But the decision to restrict the housing programme should never have been made without first discovering the number of old and infirm people who have to carry their drinking water up rickety stairs or walk to their outside lavatories through rain and snow and ice; the number of chronically sick for whom doctors cannot even claim accommodation that is dry and sanitary; the number of labourers in whose homes there is no bath. This is the kind of thing that is meant by obsolescence in housing.

For want of a public inquiry, research workers at four universities have been investigating housing conditions with the assistance of the Joseph Rowntree Memorial Trust. Without the results of their investigations this book would have been a good deal more difficult to write. I thank David Donnison, professor of social administration at L.S.E., for the opportunity to see the Rowntree Study's interim report at proof stage; Cadbury Brothers for the opportunity to see at proof stage a report on housing conditions among their workers; and both David Donnison and Malcolm Andrews, A.R.I.B.A., for help in getting the facts right.

Sources I have drawn on without acknowledgement in the text include: *Housing*, the journal of the Institute of Housing; *Housing Review*, published by the Housing Centre Trust; *Town and Country Planning*, published by the Town and Country Planning Association; *Architectural Design; The Architectural Review; The Architects' Journal; The Economist; Observer; The Times; Guardian; Daily Telegraph; Daily Herald; Evening News; Worthing Herald.*

This book treats of England and Wales. (Housing problems in Scotland and Northern Ireland are more serious still.) More often than not 'houses' must be read to mean houses and flats. The invariable use of 'dwellings' would have been tedious without being accurate, since dwellings include caravans and caves.

S.A.

1 New Houses

EVERYONE knows there is a housing shortage, but not everyone is clear about its nature. To have said this in the early post-war years would have been absurd. At the time of the 1951 Census there were 13,117,868 private households (that is, separate families) in England and Wales, but only 12,079,712 private dwellings. This disparity of 1,038,156 was the measure of the overcrowding that everyone had either experienced or observed. There were families living in lodgings, with parents, or with friends, for want of the physical availability of separate homes. The 1961 Census, however, gives 14,702,823 private households and 14,647,922 private dwellings, an excess of households over dwellings of only 54,901; and it is not to be assumed that every private household wants its own home. To allow for people moving, there should be a few per cent more dwellings than families wanting them. Even so, as measured by the national statistics, the housing shortage could be completely eradicated by one more year's building. Yet we know there are people earning well above the minimum wage who are actually homeless.

In a literal sense, the housing shortage is regional only. The Census divides England and Wales into ten regions. In nine of the ten there are more dwellings than households. The exception is the London and south-eastern region, where there are 3,666,739 households and only 3,446,551 dwellings – 220,188 fewer. Of course, as the national figures conceal regional variations, so the regional figures conceal local variations. J. Parry Lewis analysed the local-authority areas in England and Wales that had more than 7,000 dwellings in April 1961. The local variations did not in fact detract greatly from the impression given by the regional figures. In well over half the 400-odd areas outside London the number of dwellings exceeded the number of households by at least 1·5 per cent. To allow for people moving, one wants an excess of dwellings over households of nearer 3·5 per cent, which he found in only a seventh of the areas, but the disparity between an excess of 1·5 per cent and one of 3·5 per cent is not enough to cause concern. In London, on the other hand, over a third of the nearly ninety local-authority areas had less than nine dwellings for every ten households, and less than one area in five had any excess of dwellings. The fact that houses cannot be moved has perhaps more to do with the shortage than is generally recognized. At the same time, we know that the greater part of the country is not prepared to be told it has no housing shortage.

The explanation is that many people are dissatisfied with the houses they have. Their houses are decayed, dilapidated, dirty, ugly, without baths, without flush lavatories, perhaps without kitchens. They feel entitled to better houses than the ones they have. Housing does not come in the same category as medical services and education. People expect to have to pay for it. Equally they expect to be able to buy it. Belief in a minimum wage would be meaningless if there were not implicit in it the notion that it would pay for adequate food and reasonable housing.

But what is reasonable? Perhaps we can blame the housing shortage on a demand for higher standards. Undoubtedly standards have gone up. Despite the war's half million houses destroyed and $3\frac{1}{2}$ million damaged, the nation is better housed today than in 1939. But whereas before the war many families were accustomed to live in one room, they now live in three-bedroomed houses or two-bedroomed flats – in which it is axiomatic that there is no longer room for widowed parents, for whom other homes must be provided. Here of course we are dealing with the fact that houses take a long time to build. If standards in washing powders suddenly rise, the old washing powders can be completely replaced on the market in a matter of months. It would need great resolution to replace all the houses in use in fifty years.

The problem inherent in changing standards and unchanging houses has been exacerbated by housing policy. We have subsidized new housing and we have controlled the rents of old. Moreover, we have done so in arbitrary ways. We have allocated subsidized housing not, for the most part, according to people's incomes, but according to how long ago they last moved from one district to another and when they bothered to put their names on a waiting list. We have controlled private rents not only according to the value of properties but also according to when they were built. The result is that, of two men doing the same job on the same factory bench for the same earnings, one may have a shining new council house with every amenity while the other is living in an unofficial slum without even the prospect of moving. If both were living in slums, neither might be aware of a housing shortage.

There are less subtle reasons for the housing shortage. Between 1951 and 1961 the population increased by 2,313,716 or 5·3 per cent, from 43,757,888 to 46,071,604 (and it has kept on increasing faster than expected, thus upsetting all the long-term plans). With a higher standard of living people are living much longer: despite a higher birth rate, 11·9 per cent of the population are now over sixty-five, compared with only 10·9 per cent in 1951. In addition, a higher standard of living means not only that people want better housing but that they get married

younger, and that, even before they are married, the young
feel able to afford separate accommodation. Between 1951
and 1961 the number of households increased by no less
than 1,584,955 or 12·1 per cent – from 13,117,868 to
14,702,823. This is to say that during those ten years, for
every house built for a household that needed one in 1951,
another house had to be built for a new household that was
formed after 1951.

It might seem from this that improvements in the social
services and increases in the standard of living are self-
defeating. We are spending money on subsidies for housing
for the old as a direct result of spending money on medical
services and public hygiene to deter them from dying. In
part this argument needs to be met by changes in policy
appropriate to the changed conditions. With better health
and greater longevity, people are capable of working
longer and we should encourage them – or at any rate allow
them – to do so. We should then get more production from
them – a greater return on the investment in their education
and training. In general, however, there is already a return
on the expenditure on the social services, even if it is not
demonstrable in figures. Better medical services mean better
health throughout working lives. Better education means
a working population capable of doing more difficult and
more productive jobs. Better housing increases mobility
of labour and contributes both to better health and, by
providing suitable conditions in which to study, better
education. It is only because housing is regarded as a social
service that large families – which is to say families with
growing children – do, by and large, occupy the largest
houses.

The remaining causes of the housing shortage are economic and political. Council tenants have been affected by
reduced housing subsidies, high interest rates, and high land
prices. High interest rates and high land prices have also

affected owner-occupiers and private tenants. Private tenants have been affected by the Rent Act. We shall consider all these causes in subsequent chapters. Here we shall consider building costs, a factor that affects all forms of housing. It is undisputed that, relative to manufacturing industry, building suffers from a lack of technological and managerial progress.

WHY BUILDING COSTS HAVE ROCKETED

Some of the firms building houses in vast redevelopment schemes lose money, while the property companies they are working for make fortunes. Some of the biggest and most efficient firms in the industry refuse to touch housing at all. Tendering in building is truly competitive. A building firm cannot add a large percentage to its estimate to provide for unforeseen circumstances, and then gaily double it because it wants to undertake research and development. Nor, even among reasonable clients, does it get much sympathy for its increasing costs.

Building is like coalmining, in that the work it requires is hard and dirty. In addition, building labour is required to be fairly mobile. With full employment, high wages have to be paid to attract workers; and it is difficult to attract the best workers at any price. During recent years labour has organized to exploit its own shortage; in London only the influx of Irish and West Indian workers has prevented wages (and prices) from getting completely out of control. With labourers earning almost as much as bricklayers and plasterers, there is little incentive for the young recruits to the industry to take apprenticeships, and it becomes increasingly difficult to find bricklayers and plasterers. The answer to the problem lies in mechanization, which costs money. Without mechanization it is difficult to make much money, and even firms that possess or could raise the capital have been reluctant to invest it because of uncertainty about the future.

It may appear that the building industry has enjoyed one long boom since 1945, and that its confidence should be high. It remains, however, more vulnerable than most industries to fluctuations in the economy as a whole. It is also more liable than most to suffer from political decisions (such as reductions in subsidies or in the building of New Towns) and from direct political interference (such as planning decisions and the introduction of building licences). It seems also to have suffered since the war from miscalculation by Chancellors of the Exchequer in exercising their proper function of applying restrictions in order to bring booms under control. As often as not the restrictions have only begun to take effect when the industry would have been experiencing a setback anyway, and have aggravated it. New indices of production for the industry have been worked out. What the industry needs now is an assurance that if the boom in private housing comes to an end its capacity will be used for public housing.

Progress there has been. Both output and productivity have increased. One can see and hear the evidence of mechanization on many building sites, and in addition to the heavy stuff there are all kinds of refinements such as mechanical concrete finishers and mechanical plasterers. New labour-saving uses have been found for old materials (notably concrete), and new materials are being introduced at a rate of more than 200 a year. In seeking to make its actual labour force more productive, the National Federation of Building Trade Employers is giving a lead to other employers' associations. Starting with the advantage that demarcation between trades has always been less rigid in building than in engineering and shipbuilding, it is moving tactfully towards a reform of the apprenticeship system. It aims either to reduce the period of apprenticeship from five to three years, or, better, to keep it at five but let apprentices be trained in two or more allied trades, such as bricklaying, masonry, plastering, and tiling. Most important of all – for there is no doubt that standards of craftsmanship have fallen – it proposes that craftsmen who have actually passed the examinations taken at the end of their apprenticeship should automatically be given higher pay and status than those who have not. Those who have entered professions or the like may not realize how revolutionary a proposal this is. At present, in any British industry, a man is classified as skilled merely by virtue of having served an apprenticeship. If a man has not served an apprenticeship, then, no matter what knowledge or dexterity he may be able to demonstrate, he is unskilled.

Unfortunately, the behaviour of the building industry in its collective capacity is not the same thing as the behaviour of individual firms. What is wrong with the industry is that the managerial revolution has passed it by. There are a few large firms whose methods and outlook compare with those of the typical manufacturing firm. For the rest, building firms are mostly run by men who have invested their own money in them. Many are undercapitalized and depend on extended credit. Not a few are never far from bankruptcy. Whereas the professional manager's attitude is that money is always available if a way can be found to produce a good return on it, the small builder looks for a return on his own limited capital. He tries to keep his costs down by doing everything himself. In particular he tries to keep his office staff – his 'overheads' – down, regarding them as unproductive. If his profits make expansion possible, he will still be reluctant to invest in specialists – an estimator, a surveyor, an accountant – who could both improve the firm's efficiency and leave him free to concentrate on general management. He will take on more operatives and perhaps an extra clerk. The work he attempts to do himself goes up almost in proportion to the contracts he takes on. Even if in desperation he takes on a partner, the two of them will not specialize. They will just divide the work up between them. This is how even the medium-sized firms continue to have the faults of the small ones. Mr Cecil A. Francis, of the Advisory Service for the Building Industry, writes: 'Three brothers inherit a firm from their father, and all have their own particular set of customers. Three firms within a firm. There is, in fact, one very large firm, now in its fourth or fifth generation, where there are ten firms running under one title. What is possibly worse is that each director has his own pet way of going about things.'*

Since this is how the directors behave, it is not surprising that inefficiency is found at junior managerial levels. Of the man whom directors call a general foreman, but who is in practice a site manager, Mr Francis writes that he 'will be expected to be sufficiently knowledgeable on ten to a dozen crafts, labour officer, welfare superintendent, production engineer, planning officer, taker-off, specialist on safety, administrative supervisor, and public relations officer. On many sites he may also have to be a skilled mechanic and an expert on bonus systems. The fact that he has had little, if any, training on these subjects is ignored'.

In principle builders believe in progress. They support the advisory services on management and technology that are provided centrally by the industry. Just because their need for these services is so great, they can scarcely find the time to make use of them. Mr Francis tells that many of the management courses run by the Advisory Service for the Building Industry are almost ruined by firms telephoning on Friday afternoon to say: 'Mr X is sorry he is very busy and will not be able to attend next Monday.' It is the same with technology. Builders are right to be sceptical of the 200

* 'High Yield from Investment in Management,' *Building and Contracting; A Financial Times Survey*, 13 November 1961.

new materials that appear every year. Some of them are no good. Because there are so many, the Building Research Station gets behind in testing them, and in any case materials may take five years of weathering before they show their weaknesses. But scepticism does not explain the neglect of new methods. A builder may seek advice on the best solution of a problem he has encountered and so be brought face to face with one or other of the marvels of modern technology; he can avoid almost indefinitely the knowledge about how to do better the things he already knows how to do.

Housing is the province of small and medium-sized firms. School building, office building, and factory building have all benefited much more from managerial and technological progress. The greatest saving to be made in both building costs and building time is in the standardization of parts. Here progress has been slow enough in all forms of building, and slowest in housing. The problem is simple to state. The production of standardized parts is economic only on a large scale; no one wants to invest in the plant and equipment necessary to produce them without being sure they will be sold; no one wants to commit himself to buying them until he has seen what they look like – and what they look like when converted into buildings.

A start has at last been made in housing, following the example set in school building by the CLASP organization. CLASP is a Consortium of Local Authorities Schools Programmes. It comprises a number of counties, led by Nottingham, which by cooperating – by combining their demand – have developed economical prefabricated parts that can be put together on the site by any builder. Another three local authorities – Sheffield, Hull, and Leeds – are now coordinating their housing programmes with a view to standardizing parts. Flatlets for old people at Stevenage New Town have just been built with prefabricated parts –

including a steel frame that makes possible the early erection of the roof, and thus affords covered working. Meanwhile both the Building Research Station and the British Standards Institution are working (whether cooperatively or competitively is not entirely clear) on dimensional systems wherein standardization and variety may best be combined.

Talk of standardization always provokes fear of monotony in appearance. Standardization of parts has been carried much farther elsewhere in Europe, and there are some extremely standardized blocks of concrete flats to show for it. But we also know that standardized houses can be built with units as small as bricks. The parts designed for the CLASP organization – walls, columns, beams, partitions – can be and have been put together in many different ways. It is also true that in making large standardized parts it can be economic to use certain materials that would be uneconomic in the manufacture of small parts. Because of this, standardization *per se* can lead to variety. Standardized parts offer our only hope of relieving the housing shortage quickly. While they are open to abuse, they also offer one of our best hopes of a more interesting architecture.

WHAT STANDARDS WILL THE AFFLUENT SOCIETY DEMAND?

What do people want? What can they afford? These are the questions that have to be answered in determining the future standards of houses, motor cars, washing powders, or anything else. At present we know far less about the houses than about the motor cars and washing powders people want. Any wide-awake commercial firm pays a great deal of attention both to research and development and to market research. Research and development involve finding new ways of satisfying man's wants. Market research involves finding out more about the wants themselves. The

market research in housing has been even more inadequate
than the research and development. There are houses being
erected now which will give dissatisfaction to their first
occupants and in ten years will be regarded as substandard.
Probably the only organization producing houses that has
followed anything like the practice of a commercial firm
producing manufactured goods is the architect's department of the L.C.C. Fortunately things are improving. The
research and development organizations mentioned in the
previous section are partly concerned with market research,
and the Ministry's own research and development group,
consisting of architects, sociologists, and administrators, has
got down to thoroughgoing pilot surveys before introducing
new schemes.

The question of what people can afford is bedevilled by
the intricate system of subsidies in operation, but in this
context we may ignore it. We can say that the community
can at present afford the kinds of houses it is putting up on a
large scale – the small three-bedroomed house and the
rather smaller flat. Looking into the future, we have to fear
increasing prices in land and building costs, which can reduce standards. On the other hand we can look forward
optimistically to savings in costs, to higher incomes from
which people will want to spend more on housing, and,
with judicious encouragement, to a willingness for people
to spend a higher proportion of their incomes on housing.
Because houses last such a long time – say eighty years – we
have to give thought to what the standards of the future will
be. If everyone were going to expect a four-bedroomed
house in ten years' time, then by the 1970s the vast majority
of our housing would be obsolete or substandard, and the
housing shortage would be more acute than it is today
Everything turns on standards. If we reduced our
standards sufficiently, we could solve our present shortage
overnight.

There can of course be no going back on the three-bed-roomed house. Nor in practice can there be any great advance on it in the near future. As we shall see, it is going to take us long enough to bring all housing up to this standard. Fortunately standards in the number of rooms have of necessity to rise in jumps; and we have just had a jump. We can probably hold them where they are for some decades ahead. The problem narrows down to how the three-bedroomed house can be radically improved by the expenditure or by the saving in costs of perhaps another couple of hundred pounds. Many answers have been offered. The most encouraging, because they have official backing, are those embodied in *Homes for Today and Tomorrow*, published by the Stationery Office for the Ministry of Housing and Local Government in 1961. This is the report of the permanent Central Housing Advisory Committee to the Ministry, which contains architects, builders, sociologists, housewives, and medical officers, and has taken evidence from local authorities and visited housing schemes all over the country. It has the merits both of understanding the affluent society and of being sensitive to the aspirations of architects.

Affluence means by definition more possessions – not only motor cars, bicycles, prams, refrigerators, and washing machines, but more clothes, more of the tools and equipment associated with hobbies. The report recommends provision for one car per house (or flat) with extra provision for visitors; space for the new kitchen gadgets and a bit more space for those still to be invented; more electric socket outlets; more cupboards; more storage space generally. An affluent society will expect and should be allowed, not to say encouraged, to be more concerned with individual privacy and quiet. There should be more children and young people wanting to study, more adults wanting to read. The main requirements here, apart from far better soundproofing in flats, are bigger and more attractive play spaces for young children outside, and proper heating systems extending through all or most of the rooms. At present most rooms in most houses are unused most of the time because they are cold.

Even while recommending slightly larger houses, the report declares that flats should be as big as houses. After all, it argues, people living in flats have no gardens of their own and if anything are entitled to more space. It is an agreeable thought that, if flats are to be bigger anyway, we shall perhaps see more blocks of maisonettes, in designing which architects have more scope and are better able to avoid monotony. The only reason flats have been made smaller than houses is that they are more expensive to build. Certainly they should be as large if, as is true in many places, we wish to encourage people to live in them. Either economies must be found – and there is more scope for reducing the costs of flats than of houses – or financial inducements must be offered to people to live in them. Here is a rare case where it is fair to subsidize the dwelling rather than the occupier.

The recommendations about kitchens are interesting: not only should they have room for gadgets, be designed for efficient working, and have adequate drainers and worktops, but there should be room in them for people to sit down to meals comfortably. This is the result of market research by the Ministry's research and development group. The aim of architects replacing slum or near-slum property with new housing has avowedly been to get people out of the kitchen. Helped no doubt by the advent of television, they have essentially succeeded. In *The Worker in an Affluent Society*,* Dr Ferdynand Zweig reports a wife who said: 'In the other house the front room was never used except for Christmas. If I lit a fire in the front room, we always seemed

* Heinemann, 1961.

to go back into the kitchen. I suppose we were used to it.' A shop steward told him: 'In the previous house the front door was never meant to be used; we had a settee across it. Everyone, including the postman, called at the back door. Now it is different. We've moved to the front.' The sociological significance of the move to the front is not to be underestimated. The architects have done well. Yet in the last analysis the consumer has asserted his sovereignty. The Ministry's research and development group found that, even where an architect had deliberately left no room for eating in the kitchen, people had managed to force a table and chairs into it in order to eat some of their meals there. Probably the only people who never eat in their kitchens are those barred from them by servants.

The most radical thing about the report is its rejection of minimum room sizes. In their place it substitutes 'minimum overall sizes for the dwelling related to the size of family'. This is how to maintain standards while leaving to the architect the scope and authority that are properly his. We can expect now to get away from the rigid standardization that we have seen in the design of small houses since the war. Not only will there be different proportions between rooms. There will be more 'through units' – kitchens opening into dining-rooms, dining-rooms opening into living-rooms. With greater storage space to be accommodated, there will be more houses with bigger ground floors than first floors, and terraces at first-floor level; and there will be variety in the shapes of roofs.

Or will there? For the report, if it offers new scope, cannot guarantee that advantage will be taken of it. Not all that is wrong with the houses erected since the war can be attributed to restrictive standards. Even within those standards, very much better design was possible than was generally achieved. This reflects less on our architects than on those who employ them, and, in particular, those who fail to employ them. The crux of the report comes in paragraph 21, and there is nothing original in it:

The belief that the design of homes is a job that anyone can tackle with success is entirely without foundation — it is one of the most difficult tasks in the whole field of architecture. Our recommendations are made on the basis that architects must be employed as the designers of houses, and are framed in such a way as to allow for the wide variety of circumstances and site conditions confronting designers, and to leave them free either to develop conventional plan forms or to explore new living arrangements to suit changing needs.

ARCHITECTS AND LAYMEN

Architecture is a profession. And that is half the trouble. Architecture does not have to be a profession in the sense that medicine does. We do not need to be assured that an architect will get out of bed in the middle of the night in order to design a cottage for an old lady even though she cannot pay his fee. Nor does an architect have any confidences to keep which require of him more discretion than the business man. Architecture has been made a profession in an attempt to raise the status and competence of those designing buildings, and hence to raise the standards of buildings. The intention was admirable. That the attempt has failed is arguably shameful. There is, however, no virtue in denying that it has failed.

Not only do houses continue to be designed by people without qualifications. By insisting on their professional status, those who do have qualifications restrict their own power and influence. As professional men, they are not allowed to invest their own money in any concern by which they are employed or from which they receive commissions; and they may not become directors of firms of developers or builders. Thus their professional status does not restrict them in working for the State, but restricts them greatly in working for firms. In firms they must forever be subordinates; power can be wielded only by non-architects. It is no coincidence that most of the best housing has been put up by local authorities or the development corporations of the New Towns.

Already practice is rather different from theory. There are architects who are effective directors of building firms and property-development companies, and some of them have their own money invested in them. Fancy titles can be invented, and investments made in wives' names. Alternatively an architect can simply resign from the R.I.B.A. In doing so he gains his freedom and loses virtually nothing. Everyone knows that he is still as qualified as when he belonged to the R.I.B.A. He has betrayed no oath. He has not even betrayed his calling. The incentive behind many of the resignations has been to gain the power to produce more and better architecture, rather than to make more money.

It is inevitable that the R.I.B.A. will eventually waive the restrictions on its members. The sooner it does so the better. The managerial revolution will have to come to the building industry before all the potential benefits are realized, but the deprofessionalization of architecture could help to bring it. The present time is propitious for a reason noted in *Homes for Today and Tomorrow*:

Whether or not some building societies are conservative, buyers are much less so; and it is a fact worth recording that many builders have been surprised to find that houses catering for the present way of life, and conformable with the modern eye for good design, displace from their order-books older and more conventional plans which they had previously been offering . . . For design now sells; and if other considerations do not appeal, that alone should provide the incentive.

We touch here on the crucial question of public taste. Architecture is the least understood of all the arts, whereas, because it impinges on everyone, it should and could be the least esoteric. Educational reformers already have in their programme something called civics, which is to include both practical instruction in how to mark a ballot paper and write a cheque, and theoretical instruction in how Parliament and the banking system work. The reformers might start thinking up a name for another new subject, to include practical instruction in how to buy and paint a house and theoretical instruction in the essential principles of planning and design. If the theoretical instruction amounted to nothing more profound than indoctrination with films showing good architecture and commentaries that concentrated on function, treating aesthetics in painless parentheses, it would still do a great deal of good.

This is not a problem solely for secondary modern schools, but for grammar and public schools as well. People with views on Picasso, Ionesco, and Bartok still have to be told what they like in architecture. In the weeklies and the Sunday newspapers the art criticism is not written by painters and sculptors, the theatre criticism by playwrights or actors, the music criticism by composers or conductors; but the architectural criticism is for the most part written by architects. Needless to say, this is unhealthy for architects. On hearing lay praise of one of his buildings an architect does not think 'Thank God, I'm a success,' but 'This is an encouraging indication that appreciation of good architecture is spreading.' Reyner Banham, of *The Architectural Review*, has said:

Architects, buried in the convoluted coils of their complicated professional mystery, obtain little worthwhile information on the quality of the service they are offering; their horizons are often no wider than the edges of their drawing-boards, simply because the activity on the drawing-board is in itself engrossing enough for any normal mind. An outside voice that could compel their attention, and direct it to problems and values they might have overlooked, would be doing a service to both parties. If that same voice could also interpret the mysteries of the profession to laymen with equal authority, we would be in sight of an ideal situation in architectural criticism.*

The ideal he holds out amounts only to what is common-place in other forms of art criticism, yet its achievement will probably represent the last stage in establishing communication between architects and laymen. The first stage must consist in some meeting of minds between architects and builders, and in this context the emphasis must be not on more beautiful buildings but on cheaper and more quickly-erected ones. It is extraordinary how even architects them-selves, in their attacks on pre-war speculative building, implicitly concede the builders' claims that, whatever this lacked in looks, houses could not have been put up as cheaply or as quickly by any other means. An architect would have needed only five minutes to revise the down-stairs hall and the 'two rooms and a box' upstairs, to give better value for money in space. Architects cooperating with builders could have designed economical prefabricated parts even with the pre-war materials. It was of course cooperation between architects and builders in the CLASP organization which produced prefabricated parts for school building. It is to such further cooperation – particularly be-tween managerially revolutionized builders and deprofes-sionalized architects – that we must look both for more and better housing. It will manifest itself in standardization of parts, in better plans, in revision of the training given to craftsmen to take account of modern materials and methods – in a hundred different ways.

* *Listener*, 4 January 1962.

When all this has been done, we still may not like the buildings we get. You cannot please all of the people all of the time, not even if they all get the same indoctrination at school. The most we can hope to do is so to reform the present system that at least all or most of the building going up is serious architecture. If most of the theatres are performing Ionesco when one prefers Sartre – or vice versa – one has to shrug one's shoulders. But it is worth complaining if most of them are performing *Charley's Aunt*.

2 Old Houses

So FAR we have concentrated, like housing policy after the war, on the building of new houses. However fast new houses are put up, most people will always be living in non-new ones; and it is these which will determine the general standard of housing. It is the state of the non-new houses in Britain at present which is the crux of the housing problem.

At the end of the war half a million houses had been destroyed or were uninhabitable, a quarter of a million had been badly damaged, and 3¼ million damaged to some degree. There was a scarcity of building materials, and two-thirds of the building labour force were in the Services. Squatters began to take over empty flats, hotels, and service camps. The Government first requisitioned houses and used compulsory purchase to acquire sites on which to erect pre-fabricated houses. Then it turned its attention to erecting permanent houses as rapidly as possible, working through the local authorities, to whom it granted generous subsidies, and keeping strict control over materials. Rent control was preserved. Existing houses changed hands at fancy prices, even the old ones on which building societies give mort-gages only grudgingly. The repair of war damage apart, little thought was given to the maintenance of existing houses.

In the first eight years after the war, first under a Labour and then under a Conservative Government, official policy was to build as many new houses as possible. In its *Housing Programme for 1947* the Labour Government estimated that

240,000 houses would be built during the year. With a balance-of-payments crisis on its hands, it reduced its ambitions to 200,000 houses a year. House-building requires imports of soft woods, as well as stimulating the demand for other building materials and for household goods. These figures referred to Britain as a whole. We are concerned with England and Wales, where there was only one year under the Labour Government when as many as 200,000 houses were completed – 206,405 in 1948. In 1951, its last year of office, only 171,903 houses were completed.

The Conservatives came to power on a promise to build 300,000 houses a year in Britain. By allowing imports to increase, by offering even bigger subsidies, and by reducing the size of houses, the Conservatives kept their promise triumphantly. There was one year in which 300,000 houses were completed in England and Wales alone – 308,952 in 1954. An important change in policy under the Conservative Government – determined in part by its political outlook, but in part also by reduced scarcity – was the steady removal of controls. Private builders increasingly put up houses in their own right, instead of as local authorities' agents. In 1951 there were 141,587 houses completed by local authorities and 21,406 by private builders. In 1954 the figures were: local authorities 199,642; private builders 88,028. By 1961 they were: local authorities 92,880; private builders 170,366.

In the mid-1950s the Government took action to keep building down to 300,000 houses a year. It announced that the housing subsidies were to stop. Interest rates were raised. Local authorities were forced to borrow on the open market, and were told to improve their finances by increasing their rents – by subsidizing, as Mr Sandys told an outraged Opposition in the House of Commons, 'only those tenants who require subsidizing, and only to the extent of their need'. House-building fell steadily, down to 241,525

B

houses (in England and Wales) in 1958. (It has since risen again: 268,892 houses were completed in 1961.)

Whatever one may think of the original promise to build 300,000 houses a year, and of the abrupt changes that occurred once it had been kept, there is no doubt that the Government's reappraisal of housing policy was both necessary and substantially correct. Heed was at last given to the warnings of the Central Housing Advisory Committee, of professional associations, and of academics studying housing administration, that neglect of the existing stock of houses would lead to disaster. It was recognized too that council housing offered no help to those with the greatest need. Those with the smallest incomes could not afford even the subsidized rents. They were living, and would continue to live, in the older private rented property, and this was steadily decaying. It was also true that other forms of building – hospitals, schools, office blocks, and factories – had been too long neglected.

As the Government's policy has developed since its great reappraisal, it has become even clearer that it is concentrating on the replacement and improvement of the worst of the existing stock of houses. When it abolished the general-needs subsidy (i.e. subsidies for ordinary housing) it provided special subsidies for slum clearance and for flats for old people – who occupy more than their fair share of the worst housing. It first modified rent control, to allow landlords to charge higher rents if they made improvements, then set about abolishing rent control altogether, in order to allow market forces to bring about both automatic rent increases and automatic improvements. The giving of grants to property-owners for improvements was extended and simplified – with the result that grants made for improvements rose from 30,545 in 1958 to 123,447 in 1961. Because many old houses had fallen into decay for no other reason than that the building societies would not grant adequate mortgages on them, £100 million was allotted to be granted in loans (through the building societies) on houses built before 1919. (This scheme, introduced in 1959, was suspended at the time of the 'little Budget' in the summer of 1961. By then most of the £100 million had in fact been used up.)

During the last few years recognition has been growing, both among politicians and in the country at large, that millions of the houses now inhabited are beyond repair, let alone improvement. Obsolete in construction, rotten in structure, they need to be pulled down before they fall down. The idea of 'urban renewal' is novel only because we have been behaving unnaturally for so many years past. Just as new motor cars are always coming on and old ones off the roads, so the natural thing is always to be putting up new houses and pulling down old ones. All things being equal, the difference between the number going up and the number coming down should be no greater than the increase in the number of households. Since the First World War, however, we have been putting up houses pretty well as fast as we could and scarcely pulling any down at all. We have in fact put up between 7,000,000 and 8,000,000 and pulled down about 700,000. So far from taking special precautions to preserve the old houses we kept up, from 1939 to 1954 we virtually forbade major repairs. Moreover, it was only in 1919 that we laid down anything like reasonable standards for houses; and nearly half the houses inhabited today were built before 1919.

At present there is a fear in the building industry that the boom may soon burst. It would be preposterous if the building industry languished while there were so many old and decayed houses needing to be rebuilt. But it could happen. Many of these houses are in areas where there is little or no profit in rebuilding – and the rehousing of the slum-cleared is beyond the scope of the private developer. With a little foresight, however, we could seize the opportunity afforded by overcoming the physical shortage of houses, to start overcoming the shortage of good houses.

THE SLUMS

Sir Percy Rugg, Conservative leader in the L.C.C., suggested a temporary ban on large-scale slum clearance until the problem of the homeless was solved. This is an example of how a new and acute problem tends to be given precedence over a chronic one, however severe. Morally there would be as good a case for leaving all the homeless in Newington Lodge until the slums were cleared. We still have thousands of houses that were condemned as slums in the 1930s.

The slum-clearance programme begun in 1930 accounted for the demolition of 341,000 houses. When the war broke out and the programme was abandoned, houses were being demolished at the rate of 90,000 a year. The current slum-clearance programme does not even aspire to this figure, and the present rate is only 60,000. Given that we still have nearly 7,000,000 houses built before 1919, and given the introduction of reasonable minimum standards, one may safely say that slums are being created at a rate a good deal faster than 60,000 a year. The Government is not entitled to imply that its slum-clearance programme is a means of improving the country's housing.

The officially defined slums are not a special problem. By this I do not mean merely that a line has to be drawn somewhere: that the house which just gains classification as a slum is little different from the house which just escapes it. I mean that the line is not a straight one: that what is classified as a slum in one area passes for a house in another. The local authorities were asked by the Government to prepare their own estimates of the houses in their areas

which were unfit for habitation. Between them they identified 853,076 – of which they aspired, within five years from
1955, to demolish 377,878 and to patch up 88,282 for temporary accommodation. But adding the various local authorities' estimates together in this way is meaningless as a
measure of the problem. Not only did different authorities
start with different notions of unfitness – different interpre-
tations of the nebulous statutory definition. Some started
with no notion at all. They calculated how many houses
they could afford to replace over the next so many years,
and called that number slums. J. B. Cullingworth writes in
his *Housing Needs and Planning Policy*:

> To those who know Lancashire there is something odd in the
> fact that though 43 per cent of the houses in Liverpool are esti-
> mated to be unfit, the proportion in Manchester is 33 per cent; in
> Oldham 26 per cent; in Salford 24 per cent; in Bolton 10 per cent
> and in Stretford 0·5 per cent. It is true that Liverpool and Man-
> chester have appalling conditions, but they are not so markedly
> different in proportion to those in some of the other towns.*

The 1960 Report of the Ministry of Housing and Local
Government declares of the first five years of the slum-
clearance programme:

> In the event, local authorities had, by the end of 1960, dealt
> with nearly 260,000 houses and had rehoused about 750,000
> people. Although this falls short of the target they set themselves,
> it is nevertheless an impressive achievement. In many areas the
> job has been done, or at any rate reduced to small proportions;
> in others, where unfit houses are concentrated in great numbers,
> good progress has been made with both clearance and redevel-
> opment.†

* Routledge & Kegan Paul, 1960. See also Raphael Samuel, James
Kincaid, Elizabeth Slater, 'But Nothing Happens', *New Left Review*,
January–April 1962, from which I have drawn the examples in the
preface.

† H.M.S.O., Cmnd 1435, 1961.

Having declared the programme a success, the Report proceeds to give two reasons why it failed:

First, the approved proposals were optimistic about the speed with which slum clearance could be restarted, and the time which would be needed for the programme to gather real momentum . . . Second, the burden of slum clearance is unevenly spread. Over half of the slums now remaining are concentrated in about fifty local authority areas, mainly in the North and the Midlands. But often it is where the problem is biggest that it is also most difficult to raise the levels of clearance above those already achieved. Many local authorities with numerous slum houses still to clear are faced with other extensive building commitments of various kinds. Consequently, they are usually working to the limits of their manpower resources – public health inspectors, architects, engineers, and surveyors, legal staffs, building organization, and so on – and there is no easy way of supplementing these in a prosperous and fully employed economy.

It would be difficult to provide a better-argued criticism of the financial and administrative basis of housing policy. What it comes down to is that the areas with the most slums are (by definition) the poorest areas, and hence cannot afford to replace their slums. It is not enough that they can claim the same subsidy per cleared slum as any other area. The 1961 Housing Act does a little – but only a little – to help the poorer authorities at the expense of the richer. I realize that not everyone is convinced that housing should be regarded as a social service in the full sense, but we are talking now not about housing in general, but about houses admitted to be unfit for human habitation. When houses in Sheffield were rendered unfit for habitation by gales, no one argued that Sheffield should get no more help per damaged house than towns only slightly affected by the gales. Is Manchester more responsible for its slums than Sheffield for its gales? Do we believe that the sins of the Mancunian fathers should be visited upon the children unto the third and fourth generation?

Speaking on *The Housing Problem* at the annual meeting of the British Association in September 1961, J. Parry Lewis said:

If the mill-owners of Lancashire had provided better houses a hundred years ago, the slum problem today would have been a little less acute; but the costs of our exports would have risen, and there would have been less capital for us to invest abroad. The rapid industrial growth of this nation in the last century was bought partly at the cost of inferior housing, and the nation that benefited from that growth now has a responsibility towards those towns which have paid the heaviest price. It is utterly wrong that the people who live in Manchester should have to pay such a large proportion of the cost of knocking down seventy or eighty thousand slum houses and providing alternative accommodation, especially since the very existence of these houses reduces the rateable values of what would otherwise be desirable sites.

Substandard housing, while no more clearly defined than a slum, is conceived essentially in terms of lack of amenities. The Rowntree Study showed that 3 per cent of the households in England have no kitchen sink and another 4 per cent a shared one; that 29 per cent have no bath and 6 per cent a shared one; that 6 per cent have no flush lavatory and 10 per cent a shared one; that 28 per cent have no hot-water supply. Statistics like these are essential to the study of substandard housing. They must not, however, be equated with the problem. One needs to know also how many houses lacking in amenities are falling down – and indeed how many houses in which amenities have been installed are also falling down.

If we are both to get rid of the present unfit housing and to see that less housing is used to the point of unfitness in

future, we must plan the improvement or replacement of a
mass of substandard housing that is as superior to the Government's notion of a slum as it is inferior to 10 Downing
Street. And even that the Government nearly allowed to
fall down.

HOW MANY HOUSES?

In 1961 there was a spate of estimates of the number of new
houses that would be needed over the next twenty years.
J. R. James, the Ministry's chief planner, gave a minimum
figure of 5,000,000. Speaking in the House of Commons, the
Minister allowed 6,000,000. The chief Opposition speaker,
Mr Michael Stewart, thought between 6,000,000 and
8,000,000. The Alliance Building Society, in a report entitled *The Housing Land Crisis*,* gave a firm figure of
8,000,000. In terms of houses per year, these estimates vary
from 250,000 to 400,000. The current rate is less than
270,000 a year.

So much fuss was made about the Government's achievement in building 300,000 houses in a year that to many
people estimates of 300,000 to 400,000 houses a year for
twenty years must seem preposterous. A few facts will help
put these estimates in perspective. During the years just
before the war we were regularly building over 300,000
houses a year. Today we are building fewer houses in proportion to population than Germany, Sweden, Holland,
Norway, and France. Germany is building almost twice as
many houses in proportion to population as we are. Allowance must be made for varying standards – particularly in
size – but it is abundantly clear that we should be able to
build far more houses than at present.

Estimates of the numbers of new houses needed in the
future must take account both of the likely increase in the

* 1961.

number of separate households and of the number of houses likely to be pulled down. Houses will be pulled down for various reasons besides unfitness. Some will go to make room for schools, hospitals, roads, and even open spaces. Others, themselves fit but mixed up with slums or near-slums, will go to make room for new housing schemes. Yet others, though none of them very splendid ones, will go because no one wants them. These are houses standing empty in depressed areas from which the populations are migrating.

Why have the estimates of future needs varied so much? The Alliance Building Society allowed for 200,000 new households a year, whereas most estimates are 100,000 or less. For the rest, it is the number of houses that will have to be pulled down because they are just not good enough by today's standards which is the cause of disagreement. In part disagreement arises because different estimators have different notions of what constitutes an unfit house. In part also it arises from lack of precise knowledge of the state of old houses. Much thought has been given to defining minimum standards for the new houses we are going to put up, very little to defining minimum standards for the old houses we are going to leave up. It is generally accepted that if old houses are to be left up, they should have the standard amenities installed. But flush lavatories, kitchen sinks, baths, and the like all take up space, and the rooms in many of the old houses are – by the standards set for new houses – too small to start with. What should be the minimum size of an old house complete with modern amenities? A decision could at least be reached on this question with the knowledge we already have. Because we lack precise knowledge of the state of repair of old houses, we cannot begin to say in how many of them it is worth installing amenities.

The Government's various policies have all been adapted to its ignorance of the state of old houses. It could be assumed that landlords would not repair their houses in order to charge higher rents unless they were worth repairing; that neither landlords nor owner-occupiers would apply for improvement grants (for part of the cost of installing amenities) unless they were worth improving; that money provided for mortgages on pre-1919 houses would not be wasted on useless houses, because would-be owner-occupiers would not want them (and in any case the scheme was administered by the building societies). The Government's policies have no doubt been successful in preventing houses from being repaired or improved unless they justified it.

There remains the problem of ensuring that houses are repaired and improved if they do justify it. The Government cannot even have a policy on this until the facts have been established. How many houses could be given another forty years of life if they were brought up to standard now? How many another thirty years? How many another twenty? In each case, what would it cost? Where are these houses? Who owns them? When we have the answers to these questions, we shall both know what needs to be done and be able to decide on the most suitable administrative means of ensuring that it is done.

Without knowing how many old houses it is worth preserving, we cannot say how many we shall have to pull down. The estimates made of the numbers of new houses that will be needed have had to be based on arbitrary assumptions about pulling down all the houses built before certain dates – assumptions that would theoretically involve the demolition of Blenheim Palace. The correspondence between the age of houses and their quality is inexact, but it is close enough to make possible worthwhile estimates of national needs, if not of local needs. We do not in fact know the ages of the houses now standing, but here again the estimates are reliable enough to be useful. The White

Paper* published in February 1961 dated the origins of
the 14⅓ million houses and flats in England and Wales as:

Since 1945†	3⅓ million
Between 1919 and 1940	4⅓ million
Between 1880 and 1915	3 million
Before 1880	3⅔ million

Other authorities on housing suggest that the old houses
are older still. If we base our arguments on the figures in the
White Paper, there can be no question of overestimating the
problem. Most of the houses officially recognized as slums
were built before 1880. Most of the houses built before 1880
are not officially recognized as slums. There can, however,
be comparatively few houses built before 1880 which constitute satisfactory homes today. Eighty years is a fair life for
an ordinary house – even a good house. Most of the houses
built before 1880 were not good ones. Not only had no
minimum housing standards been laid down. Until the
Public Health Act of 1875 there were no effective building
regulations. It is a safe assumption that we have 3,000,000
houses that we ought to pull down right away. It is almost
unthinkable that we should not have pulled them down
before they are a hundred years old. Suppose then we make
1978 the year in which we must finish pulling down our
worst 3,000,000 houses, and set about the job in earnest in
1963. This gives us a building rate, over fifteen years, for
replacement alone, of 200,000 houses a year. When to this
we add the moderate rate of 100,000 a year estimated as
necessary to satisfy the new households being formed, we get
a figure of 300,000 a year. We still have to allow for the
replacement of houses pulled down for other reasons than

* *Housing in England and Wales*, H.M.S.O., Cmnd 1290.
† This includes dwellings provided by conversion, as well as new
dwellings.

unfitness. And we have made no provision for pulling down any of the other 3⅔ million built before 1919 (when real housing standards were introduced).

In his Fabian pamphlet *The Housing Problem*,* John Greve presents a house-building programme for the next twenty years which shows the implications of allowing houses maximum lives of 100 years and of 75 years.

1. If all houses built before 1880 are to be replaced by 1980 – giving them a maximum life of 100 years: 200,000 *houses a year*.
2. If all houses are given a maximum life of 75 years, a more reasonable span allowing for the rise in living standards: 300,000 *houses a year*.
3. Formation of new households: 100,000 *houses a year*.
4. Miscellaneous: replacement of houses lost through redevelopment; new roads; changes in land use (more for schools, open spaces, etc.); migration from decaying areas to expanding industrial areas, causing abandonment of houses, etc.: say 25,000 *houses a year*.

Total: 325,000 to 425,000 houses a year. The current rate of building is 270,000 a year in England and Wales.

If the Government announced a programme of 325,000 to 425,000 houses a year for the next twenty years – if it set about raising production to 325,000 a year as soon as possible and aspired to raise it further thereafter – one could feel the housing problem was being tackled. But it would still be a matter of urgency to investigate the state of houses built before 1900 – all of which will be over eighty years old in another twenty years' time – and it would be wise at the same time to investigate all houses built before the First World War. A programme of repairs and improvements should then be prepared for all the old houses worth preserving. And there should be periodical investigation of the state of old houses thereafter.

* 1961.

We do not want a twenty-year plan. We want twenty-year planning. A twenty-year plan is a means of being bound by the mistaken decisions of yesterday. Twenty-year planning means anticipating the needs of the future, always on the best available evidence. One starts with a plan for the years 1963–83, which assumes, say, that 100,000 houses a year will be needed for new households, 200,000 a year for the replacement of unfit houses, and 25,000 a year for other replacements; and that so many houses a year will need and be worth repairing and improving. In 1968, say, one must produce a new plan – in practice revise the old one – for the years 1968–88; in 1973 one must produce a plan for the years 1973–93; and so on. If it appears that new households are being formed faster than has been allowed for, or that more houses are beyond repair than has been assumed, then the programme must be increased accordingly. If new households form more slowly than has been allowed for, or more houses are discovered to be worth preserving than has been assumed, then one may either reduce the programme or raise the standards one has set for the preservation of old houses; but on the assumptions we have made for our twenty-year plan, either of these possibilities is remote.

The Conservative 300,000 houses a year was a national figure. Our twenty-year plan must not deal in national figures in this sense. The national figures must be made up of house-building programmes prepared separately for different regions – programmes dependent on local need, not on local finance. This is to say that the criteria used in determining regional programmes must be not regional but national. The word 'slum' must mean the same in Bolton and Stretford as in Bournemouth. Regional plans must reflect local needs not only in the size of the building programme but in their subdivision into different kinds of housing. They must provide for the replacement of houses,

for the increase in households, and for the nature of households – whether they will be families with children, old
people, young single people. It is the regional plans that
must be revised over the years – in accordance with the
regional trends that reveal themselves. Overfulfilment of
any one regional plan would be admirable in itself, but it
should not be set against underfulfilment elsewhere in order
to declare the fulfilment of the national plan.

Finally, it is no use having plans based on all the trends
when one of the trends shows there will soon be no space in
which to build houses without abandoning whatever principles have been established about densities of population
and the preservation of open spaces. We are beyond the
point where planning can concern itself merely with seeing
that houses are built where people are going to want them.
It has to contrive that people will want them where they can
be built.

Even though we see that other countries in Europe are
building more houses than we are, a programme of 325,000
to 425,000 houses a year plus an extensive programme of
repairs and improvements may seem a tall order. Since the
Government's great reappraisal in the mid-1950s, we have
deliberately let investment in housing fall. One would like
to see this trend reversed. Since, however, we are looking
ahead over the years, we do not have to take the present
national income as given, and ask simply what expenditure
we can cut in order to have more houses. We can count not
only on increased productivity in building, but on a rising
national income from which more can be spent on housing,
both directly by individuals and indirectly through the
State and local authorities. We can try to devise policies
that will oblige or encourage people to spend a larger proportion of their incomes on housing. We can seek to keep
costs down – both building costs and, through better planning, the cost of land. In so far as we cannot keep the cost of

land down, we can tax capital gains, or levy other taxes on property, in order to give ourselves more money to play with. Put like this, the prospect looks less forbidding. This is the proper way to put it. The housing problem has twenty different sides to it and needs to be attacked on them all at once – but not without a certain amount of coordination.

LUXURY BUILDING

A discussion of how many houses a year it is possible to build should not be concluded without some mention of luxury building. If luxury building were restricted, more materials would be available for building humbler houses. That much is irrefutable. 'Luxury building shouldn't be allowed,' says the Left-wing militant, without more ado. The educated – of the Left as well as of the Right – dismiss this on the ground that it is economically unsophisticated, though most of them might be hard put to it to explain why. It merits consideration. It is not in fact only the unsophisticated and the sentimental who demand that luxury building should be restricted. J. Parry Lewis, an economist, in the same address to the British Association in which he declared that the Rent Act had done a great deal of good and that there were strong arguments for further decontrol of rents, had this to say of luxury building:

One thing that should be borne in mind is that large ostentatious houses have little justification in either social or economic terms. It has been said that every new house built enables a whole succession of moves, which eventually will leave free a house into which some slum tenant can move. But this is hardly the most efficient way of dealing with slums. The resources needed to build some houses that are more status symbols than homes could build three houses vastly better than those in which some of our industrial population now live ... There is a strong argument either for re-introducing controls, forbidding the

erection of houses above a certain size, or for taxing new houses
that cost more than a certain amount. If the builder of a new house
had to pay a 50 per cent tax on the amount by which the cost
exceeded £3,000, so that there would be a tax of £500 on a
house costing £4,000, and a tax of £1,000 on a house costing
£5,000, then the amount of extravagant building now going on
would certainly be diminished.

Even when we are reading an economist's views, it is
evident that behind the figures lie feelings of outrage. It is as
well therefore if we start from some clear premise about the
nature of the social conscience. We now have evidence, in
the work of Dr Elliott Jaques,* about the material aspects of
the social conscience – about the 'social norms' that satisfy
innate feelings of equity. Man is a strictly egalitarian animal
only at the subsistence level. The more affluent a society, the
wider the differentials that command general acceptance.
This is why Gandhi wore *khadi*, and President Kennedy has
the best-dressed wife in America. Apply the principle to
housing, and one gets the answer that luxury building is
liable to appear offensive so long as some housing is below a
minimum acceptable standard.

The Left-wing militant is always going to object to luxury
building, and his views may be dismissed as unrepresentative as well as impracticable. But the economist who wants
to restrict luxury building to speed slum-clearance cannot
be ignored. Nor, indeed, can the Presbyterian minister†
who suggested that the Queen should allow some of London's 3,000 homeless to stay in some of the 600 rooms at
Buckingham Palace. (So far from being anti-royalist, he
recalled with loyal approval how, when hot water was
scarce in wartime, King George VI restricted his baths to a
depth of five inches like everyone else.) Without wanting

* See his *Equitable Payment*, Heinemann, 1961.
† The Rev. William Barbour, of Newcastle.

Buckingham Palace requisitioned, I think there is a clear case for restricting less essential kinds of building – not only luxury house-building but also office-building – in order to carry out a crash programme both to house the homeless and clear the slums. I doubt, however, whether it is now practical politics. The opportunity was lost when popular feeling about the homeless was at its height in 1961.

Given a minimum standard of housing for all, exception can be taken to luxury building only in special cases. Since land is physically scarce, building that consumed excessive space could be a special case. But we already have the answer to this in planning powers and compulsory purchase. In practice the very large houses are mostly put up in the country, where land is not in great demand; what is classed as luxury building in the cities consists largely of blocks of flats with fairly high densities. At times when the raw materials of building are physically scarce, there is again reason to control luxury building. For the rest, luxury building is just one of the many ways in which the rich may choose to spend the money that the system of taxation decreed by a democratic legislature allows them to keep. There is always an argument for allowing them to keep less. But luxury building as such has no more significance than luxury cars and luxury dinners.

3 What Do People Want of Housing?

WE HAVE already remarked on how little reliable information there is about what people want of actual houses. The same difficulty arises when we ask the wider question: 'What do people want of housing?' The politicians do not seem concerned to know the answers. They know that householders like security of tenure, and that they dislike increases in their rents, mortgage-interest payments, or rates; and, according to party, they conceive every honest working man as aspiring to own his own house or to become a council tenant. It is true that once a man becomes either an owner-occupier or a council tenant, he is unlikely to change to a different form of tenure; but this is not the same thing.

Of the evidence available, that which lends most support to the politicians' views is Dr Zweig's study of affluent workers in six large factories. He was able to divide them into three roughly equal groups: those who tried to acquire house property; those who just did not think about house property, regarding it as something beyond their reach; and those who rejected the acquisition of house property outright as undesirable and even pernicious for the working man. But his findings taken as a whole give a different impression.

Private rented property was definitely unpopular. Even this, however, does not necessarily imply a dislike of private tenancy as such. If, in part, it reflected insecurity of tenure and a fear of higher rents in the future – which are perhaps unavoidable attributes of private tenancy – it reflected also the fact that most of the lower-priced private rented property is at present old and in a poor state of repair. The affluent workers' main desire seemed to be to have a new or modern house. Certainly the behaviour and attitudes of new owner-occupiers and new council tenants were almost identical. 'Moving to a new house, be it a council house or privately owned, starts the suburban drive of status-seeking through the home.' Owner-occupiers and council tenants alike became both house-proud and 'home-centred'. When they were not decorating their homes, buying new furniture, or digging their gardens, they were fiddling with their cars. Pubs and cinemas were neglected in favour of television.

The owner-occupiers struck Dr Zweig as 'a brighter, more daring and enterprising breed than the rest'. He felt that on the whole they cared more for freedom, whereas the council tenants cared more for security. But many of the owner-occupiers had decided to buy houses only because they knew they would have to wait years before getting a council house. And many of the council tenants may have had good reason for being concerned about security. Redundancy is after all one of the problems of our time. A man who is out of work can in necessity get rent on National Assistance almost automatically. Getting assistance with mortgage payments is less straightforward.

The fact is that it is difficult to ascertain the true preferences of the population between different kinds of tenure in the absence of a free choice. All over the country there are young married couples living of necessity in expensive lodgings or furnished rooms. If they are poor earners, poor savers, or poor birth-controllers they must hope to end up with a council house. Otherwise they may well act on a careful calculation of how they can get a house quicker – by having children (in their unsuitable accommodation), and so being moved up the waiting list for a council house; or by not having children, and so being able to save money towards buying a house.

Probably the most direct answers to the question 'What do people want of housing?' come from a survey carried out among Cadbury's workers at Bournville and Fry's workers at Somerdale, near Bristol.* This provided virtually no evidence of a desire for different kinds of tenure for their own sake, which is the more significant because the many householders on the Bournville estate who work for Cadbury's, while they are not especially affluent, have exceptional security in their jobs. They are no more representative of householders in general than Dr Zweig's affluent workers are representative of workers in general. Both are interesting because, being unrepresentative of today, they are very likely representative of tomorrow.

In the Bournville survey, householders who wished to move were asked why. Some of course gave more than one reason. The reason given most frequently (35 per cent of all informants) had nothing to do with actual houses. It was to live in a nicer neighbourhood. And it was given with roughly equal frequency by private tenants, council tenants, and owner-occupiers. The other reasons given, in descending order of frequency, were: to have more rooms; to have a bathroom; to have a place in decent repair; to have a shorter journey to work; to get a smaller house; to economize in rent. To have a bathroom was given as a reason by a large proportion of private tenants (41 per cent) and a small proportion of council tenants (7 per cent). Similarly, to have a place in decent repair was given by a large proportion of private tenants (29 per cent) and a small proportion of council tenants (8 per cent). These answers clearly reflect the generally poor condition of private rented property and the generally good condition of council property.

* See John Greve, *People and their Houses* (Cadbury Brothers, Bournville, 1962).

The fact that there are people wanting smaller houses – mostly of course old people – as well as people wanting larger houses may suggest a simple solution to both problems. With a few per cent surplus houses, some people would move out from the large houses they do not want and other people from smaller houses could then move into them. But it is not solely a question of facilitating exchanges, whether on the Bournville estate or elsewhere. Moving is a great deal of trouble, and it is expensive. The family wanting a larger house will not be prepared to move into any large house. While they are moving they will hope to move into a house in a nice neighbourhood not far from the householder's work. Similarly, old people with houses too big for them may not think it is worth the trouble to move into a smaller house or flat unless it is one adapted to their needs.

On the evidence, while most people probably have a preference as between owning their own house and being a council tenant, other considerations are usually more important. People want, of course, a house of appropriate size with modern amenities. Over and above this they are concerned to live in a nice neighbourhood. In planners' terms, a nice neighbourhood is one where the housing is generally good and the density low, where parks, playing fields, libraries, cinemas, pubs, and shops are well spaced and placed. Another important consideration to the householder is a short (and comfortable) journey to work.

The reasons people give for wanting to move do not reveal everything that is inadequate about their housing. The reasons will be limited both by what they feel is in practice attainable and by the extent to which they have analysed their needs and desires. There are surely other things they want or would like besides those we have mentioned.

COMMUNITY SENSE AND PRIVACY

The predominant movement in architecture after the war was even more Left-wing than the country at large. Architects have fewer inhibitions than most people about according powers to the State, because without planning powers they cannot hope to design decent cities and towns. They also observe the workings of the property market closely, and see money being made for nothing. Partly because of their political inclinations and associations, they reacted, perhaps excessively, to all that had been wrong with housing before the war. The 'Garden City' tradition had been much abused, and of course speculative builders had continued to erect houses in long rows following straight streets. Everywhere fences had grown higher. Community sense had been destroyed, aloofness and snobbishness fostered. A suburban householder might never even speak to his next-door neighbours. He probably did not know the names of the people living two doors away. The people who really knew how to live were the slum dwellers, sitting on one another's doorstep to chat, always ready to help one another in a crisis. The young post-war architects set out to re-create mateyness at all levels of society. They would have wanted to build cluster groups of palaces, except that they were all republicans.

While residential units – of anything up to forty houses or flats – have been advocated mainly on the grounds that they foster neighbourliness and make possible a more pleasing architectural arrangement, they do of course offer practical advantages as well. In them can be incorporated communal garages, communal playgrounds, communal utility rooms for washing and drying clothes. To make it convenient for the housewife to do her washing in her own house is possible, but requires more space than the time she spends washing really justifies. The result is that many housewives do their washing in kitchens that are too small and not intended to be got wet, and have to make lunch in the middle of it all. The popularity of launderettes is easy to understand: they are cheap; they save the muddle and mess at home; and housewives can sit chatting while their washing is being done. But the journey to the launderette can be a long one, a queue may have formed there, and housewives who are working may in any case prefer to do their washing late in the evening when the launderette is closed. A communal utility room has everything to commend it even if status-conscious housewives do insist on keeping non-communal washing machines in them.

Unqualified support for mateyness does still exist. Discussing neighbourhood units in an article in the *Guardian* on the architecture of 1961, Diana Rowntree wrote: 'The genteel terraces of the new towns have taken such a beating lately that the idea of social cohesion has annihilated the claims of space and privacy.'* In fact, however, the reaction against mateyness had already begun. There have been two reasons for it. The first is the belated recognition that slum dwellers, for all their community sense, value privacy highly. Their propensity for sitting on doorsteps to chat is explained by their reluctance to allow each other through their front doors. The second reason is that when you take people out of slums they cease to behave like slum-dwellers. With bourgeois homes – and nowadays bourgeois incomes – they develop bourgeois tastes and attitudes. In Dr Zweig's view, 'The intensity of neighbourly contacts can be graded in this order: (1) villages; (2) old-established working-class areas; (3) new estates; (4) residential quarters with own house property. The sociability on new council estates is rather low, generally speaking.'

The question is whether, even if one is able to, one should endeavour to alter this state of affairs through architecture. The sociability of the workers studied by Dr Zweig had

* 28 December 1961.

undoubtedly decreased as their affluence had increased – and had decreased in particular when they acquired new houses, whether their own houses or council houses. 'We won't be able to get rid of them if we are too friendly.' 'Do a good turn if possible, to show that you are friendly; but if you are too friendly the place is never your own.' 'Don't spoil your neighbourhood by getting too close.' These comments are but a few of the variations on 'a constant refrain that the intrusion of neighbours may restrict a man's freedom and his privacy'. It surely need surprise no one that families that are prosperous and well-housed experience a less compulsive need for social intercourse than families struggling with poverty in slums. Privation will make anyone friendlier. Even the occupants of the inter-war suburban terraces spoke to one another when they were bombed out. Among the prosperous and well-housed, the innate need for intimate social intercourse can be satisfied largely within the family. 'Family-centredness' is greatly encouraged by car-ownership and by television.

If 'friendly but not too close' are the relations householders are going to want, then 'friendly but not too close' are the relations architects should design for. By being friendly, Dr Zweig's affluent workers meant more than saying, 'Good morning'. They meant being ready to give a hand with repairing a fence, to look after a dog or cat while its owners were away, perhaps to look after children while the mothers went out. All this is a vindication of residential units, since without them one is unlikely to get enough friendliness. Given that one is designing a residential unit, however, the problem is not so much to encourage friendliness as to ensure privacy. This is being increasingly recognized. In the latest New Town, Cumbernauld, for example, the houses have been spaced with the intention of preserving privacy and care has been taken to ensure that windows do not overlook one another.

There remains the problem of transition. Take people away from the slums, and they develop bourgeois tastes and attitudes. But they do not develop them immediately. For the slum-cleared to be unhappy in their splendid new homes is commonplace, and this is a problem to which architects are still rightly seeking solutions, with some success. In a survey conducted among tenants in four buildings in the East End of London, Peter Willmott and Edmund Cooney of the Institute of Community Studies asked three questions: 'Is it easy to get to know other tenants if you want to? Have you enough privacy? Do you ever feel too cut off from others?' The L.C.C.'s four-storey maisonette blocks in Stepney produced affirmative answers of 95 per cent, 79 per cent, and 5 per cent. Another of the buildings where the survey was conducted was the cluster block in Bethnal Green, in which the architect, Denys Lasdun, had sought to recapture the sociable quality of East End streets in the central access block of lifts, stairs, chutes, and public space, while maintaining privacy in the maisonettes and flats which are approached along short access balconies. Here 100 per cent of the tenants had enough privacy, but only 29 per cent felt it was easy to get to know other tenants, and 42 per cent felt too cut off from others. On this and other evidence the Bethnal Green flats must be reckoned a social failure (though a sculptural triumph).

As part of the slum-clearance and redevelopment programme for the central area of Preston, James Stirling and James Gowan designed flats, maisonettes, and houses (in four and two storeys) which, as well as being grouped around a central space to give a sense of community, were built in the local red Accrington engineering bricks. Familiarity was enhanced by using the actual brick detailing of the cotton mills. Certainly the Stirling–Gowan scheme is peculiarly successful in preserving continuity with the slums it has displaced. It is perhaps easy for architects to become so intrigued by the problem of how to recreate the spirit of the slums that they do not stop to ask to what extent it is desirable to do so. One cannot have it both ways. The more at home the slum-cleared feel on their first day in their new flats, the sooner will their developing bourgeois tastes and attitudes make them dissatisfied with them.

Designing houses for the slum-cleared and for the rich should not be regarded as presenting problems that are different in kind, only different in degree. We need to combine the formula of 'friendly but not too close', which derives from the upper working class, with Dr Zweig's general rule of 'the higher the level of prosperity, the higher the fences'. In all housing, the privacy of the home must be inviolate, and at the same time contacts between neighbours can be fostered to varying degrees. With this reservation, the concept of the residential unit can be applied to private houses costing £4,000 or £8,000 no less than to council flats costing £2,250. It is already being applied to them. With derequisitioning many large sites suddenly became available to property-developers in the London area. On a number of them, well-designed houses have been grouped, as in the SPAN developments at Ham Common and Blackheath (architect Eric Lyons). In the Southwood House Development scheme at Highgate (architects Andrews, Emmerson, and Sherlock) forty-three houses have been built, each with its own small enclosed garden, backing on to a central space where a children's playground has been devised among the original trees.

Mateyness had not been the only concern of the post-war architects. In further emulation of the slums, they wished to create a wider community sense as well. The residential units of the slums are clearly defined – usually by intersecting streets – but they are not enclosed. The streets continue. There are contacts between adjacent residential units, and with them a community sense. The residential units make up a neighbourhood unit. The Dudley report (*Design for Dwellings*,* published in 1944) included a report of a study group on site planning and layout in relation to housing, which dealt with the principles of neighbourhood planning.

In the earlier blocks of flats in which slum-dwellers were rehoused, the only equivalent of the street was the lift-shaft or staircase – which is to say that the street became a cul-de-sac. At Bethnal Green the vertical cul-de-sac was crossed with horizontal lanes, but of necessarily limited length. In an immense slum-clearance and redevelopment scheme at Park Hill near the centre of Sheffield (City Architect J. L. Womersley) horizontal 'streets' meander at every third-floor level, being bridged from block to block, for over half a mile. In addition to being linked in this way, the residential units are related to a shopping centre, a community centre, and (though it is still to be built) a school. Like Bethnal Green, Park Hill has its faults (some of them possibly inherent in the high density), but the attempt to re-create a neighbourhood unit may well be successful. It is a fact that many of the former residents of the century-old back-to-backs – who when these were pulled down had to move to outlying council estates – have now returned to Park Hill.

Elsewhere, even in the New Towns, it has been found more difficult to create a neighbourhood unit than a residential unit. In particular, many of the actual community centres have languished. To a large extent this is because they have not provided for the right communal activities – or not for enough of them. The nearest thing to a successful community centre in the rebuilt centre of Coventry is a huge commercial dance hall. Private enterprise is coming even nearer to creating community centres proper, in the cinemas it has adapted for bingo and bowling with catering services thrown in. Competition from the communal activities organized in the church halls is also intense. But with

* This was the predecessor of *Homes for Today and Tomorrow*.

all this, the architects and planners can claim to have been unlucky. It is arguable that the community centres would have transformed the use of leisure in this country, had not television transformed it first. It is yet possible that television viewing will greatly decrease as the novelty wears off. It is also possible that as the novelty wears off the newly housed will stop repainting their walls every six months. If, for whatever reasons, people become less 'home-centred', and yet keep their relations with immediate neighbours 'friendly but not too close', then the community centres will have a chance to revive. In the long run it may appear that television has helped them, by breaking the habit of regular cinema-going and forcing many of the cinemas to close.

SECURITY AND MOBILITY

Of the kinds of security which people need and which the State can do something about, security in housing is arguably the most fundamental – better lose one's job than one's home. Yet we have not succeeded in providing security in houses, let alone in housing. To be free of anxiety about housing, people must not only be able to afford what it is costing them and feel that they can meet any possible increase in costs. They must have security of tenure; security against substantial expense if they have to move; and security against not being able to find somewhere else if they have to move, whether because of their jobs or because of contracting families or incomes. In addition, people living in a free society should be able to move to another part of the country merely because they would like to. This is a tall order only in the sense in which steak was a tall order during war-time food rationing. If food rationing had been perpetuated for nearly twenty years after the war, there would be an entire generation who had never known what eating should be, and no one who could remember clearly. Food might then almost have ceased to be a political issue, in the way that housing has. We now take it for granted that people should have all the medical treatment and all the education they want, yet neither is as fundamental as housing.

The private tenant lacks security of tenure; and if he lives in a city where increasing population is forcing up land prices, there is no limit to the rent increases that may be demanded of him even if he is allowed to stay. An owner-occupier who is declared redundant, and takes only a few weeks to find another job, will probably not be able to meet his commitments in the meantime; and the owner-occupier may always be let in for the cost of major repairs for which he has made no provision. It is no use saying he ought to save. All his savings went on the down-payment for his house and the legal costs incurred in buying it. The council tenant has the greatest security in his actual house. He is most unlikely to be evicted from it and he will virtually never be evicted from it without being offered another one. His rent is liable to be increased, but not to an extent that will cause him hardship. Against this he must set the fact that he has virtually no mobility whatever – virtually no protection against the contingency of having to take a job in another part of the country. Direct exchanges between council tenants in different areas are possible but are not to be relied on. Either the private tenant or the owner-occupier stands a reasonable chance, if he has to move, of obtaining accommodation equivalent to that which he is leaving. The council tenant will probably find himself at the bottom of some local authority's waiting list, back where he started many years ago.

Only a small proportion of the moves that are made are attributable to changes of jobs. In the Rowntree Study, a change of job was given as a reason for past moves by 42 per

cent of households whose heads were in administrative,
professional, managerial, or proprietary jobs, but by only
11 per cent of those with employed heads in other occupa-
tions. Eight per cent of those interviewed had moved during
the previous year, and of these three out of four had found a
new house within a bus ride of their old one. The main
reasons for moving are changes in domestic circumstances,
such as marriage or the birth of children, and of course the
desire for better homes. People tended to move from furnished accommodation to unfurnished privately rented property; from privately rented property to either council
housing or owner-occupied housing; or simply into better
housing of the same tenure. There was also a tendency for
new households to form in the centre of a city and then
move outwards, but this may be only another way of saying
that they form in privately rented property (mainly built
before 1914 in the centre) and then move into council
housing or owner-occupied housing (mainly built after 1919
in the suburbs).

When the housewives of established households are asked
if they want to move, they seem to think almost solely in
terms of getting a bigger or better house. There is no more
point in asking them if they want to move to another part
of the country, whether because they would prefer it or
because the employment prospects are better, than in asking
an Indian peasant if he wants to eat steak. In conditions of
housing shortage they just do not think about it. Moves
from one part of the country to another do occur. Too many
moves into the south-east present one of the problems, and
an article in the *Ministry of Labour Gazette* in June 1961
showed that mobility of labour in all directions is greater
than had been realized. But for the most part the moves
must be made by the young and single, or by established
households that have been organized into moving by employers. How much movement there ought to be – either

local or regional – we shall not even know until good housing is available all over the country.

The authors of an interim Rowntree study report say:

Our findings suggest that most of those who move find a house that suits them better than their previous one. On the whole, therefore, movement is a good thing and worth promoting for its own sake.

They emphasize the critical point that is reached as soon as there is ample housing available for new households. Established households then become much freer to move, always leaving empty houses behind them for others to move into.

Thus it may be that the high mobility of American households is due as much to their high standard of living (which includes a plentiful supply of housing) as to the cultural traditions commonly quoted in explanations of this phenomenon.*

* D. V. Donnison, Christine Cockburn, and T. Corlett, *Housing Since the Rent Act*, Codicote Press, Welwyn, 1961.

4 Owner-Occupation

WITH $6\frac{1}{2}$ million owner-occupiers among $14\frac{3}{4}$ million house-holders, the Conservative ideal of a property-owning demo-cracy is no longer derided. Since owner-occupiers increased by $2\frac{1}{4}$ million between 1952 and 1962, the sixties should see them in a majority. The Rowntree study showed that a third of skilled-manual-worker heads of households and a fifth of unskilled were owner-occupiers; and that two-thirds of new purchasers were manual workers.

We have seen that not all owner-occupiers are volunteers. A house may be bought because there is no other way of getting one to live in. The Bournville survey revealed owner-occupiers spending a third of their income on hous-ing, and one may suppose they would prefer to spend less as tenants in equivalent accommodation were it obtainable. The reduction in 1956 of the number of council houses built for general needs increased the coercion of the young mar-ried householder into owner-occupation. If there were no housing shortage, the increase in the number of owner-occupiers would at all events be less rapid.

Owner-occupation is not to be equated with enjoyment of splendid housing. Manual workers are not all buying the suburban semi-detacheds built since 1930. (Indeed, until recently these had been built mainly in the south-east, where the price of houses makes property-owning demo-cracy still remote.) The Rowntree study showed that 16 per cent of owner-occupied houses have no fixed bath, 5 per cent no hot water supply, and 6 per cent no flush lavatory.

Probably 20 per cent of owner-occupied houses were built before 1914. A survey conducted in 1959–60 by the Cooperative Permanent Building Society* (which accounts for about 5 per cent of the business transacted by the building-society movement) showed that nearly a quarter of its mortgagors bought houses costing less than £1,000. Nearly three-quarters of them bought houses costing less than £2,500.

New houses as such cost £2,500 or more (though new flats may cost less). Of the Cooperative Permanent's mortgagors who were earning less than £750, only 7·5 per cent bought houses costing more than £2,500. Slightly more than half its mortgagors earned less than £750, as do slightly more than half of industrial workers. To buy a house costing £2,500, a man earning less than £750 would normally need to make a down payment of £500 or more, as well as pay his legal expenses. If he got a mortgage for £2,000 at 6 per cent repayable over twenty-five years, and a mortgage protection policy, his mortgage interest at 6 per cent plus his premiums would cost about £140 a year. Because he was earning less than £750, a building society would not want to give him a mortgage if it meant he would spend more than a fifth of his income on housing. (It would let a man earning more spend a quarter.) An allowance for repairs and maintenance and insurance would in fact bring his outgoings on housing to more than a fifth of his income (£150 a year), but because he was making a large down payment he would probably get his mortgage. If the house was leasehold and he had ground rent to pay, however, he would almost certainly be refused. (For some reason building societies seem to ignore rates in their calculations.) For a man earning less than £750 to be able to make a down payment of £500 would in fact be unusual. (More than half the down payments made by all the Cooperative Permanent's

* *Who Buys Houses?* Occasional Bulletin No. 38, July 1960.

mortgagors were less than £300.) This would matter less if it were easy for him to buy an old house. In fact an old house, though cheaper, may mean an even larger deposit, since no building society will want to grant a large mortgage on it.

The upshot is that this country has an enormous number of people willing to devote more to housing than they are allowed to. The absurdity of the situation is tolerated only because it has come about slowly. Time was when people were able to rent houses. Then everyone became accustomed to a housing shortage attributable to physical shortage – to the destruction of houses during the war and to a scarcity of the materials necessary to build new houses. Today there is no serious scarcity of materials. We can build as many houses as we can pay for. Yet while we draw on the Exchequer to finance council housing, we do not draw on the contributions which people are willing to make voluntarily. This conflicts with common sense, let alone with the ideal of a property-owning democracy.

The advantages of extended owner-occupation are more evident in old houses than in new. We have already remarked that the council tenants among Dr Zweig's affluent workers knuckled down to painting and distempering with the same enthusiasm as the owner-occupiers. There is a contrast between the attitude of owner-occupiers and of landlords to old houses. Improvement grants were conceived as a means of encouraging landlords to install modern amenities in old property. In the event, far fewer grants have been applied for by landlords than by owner-occupiers. As J. B. Cullingworth wrote in a study of housing in Lancaster, 'Owner-occupiers are not worried about percentage returns: their concern is with comfort and convenience.'* That they are none the less concerned about the price at which their houses can be sold is a further advan-

* 'Housing and the private landlord', *Guardian*, 24 March 1961.

tage. If an owner-occupier contemplates moving, he will not, like a private tenant, be tempted to neglect his house.

Even when allowance is made for the coercion exercised by shortage, it is probably true that the average householder is ready to spend a larger proportion of his income on a house he owns than on one he rents. For the individual, owner-occupation means increased saving and security: once he has paid off a substantial part of an original mortgage he can usually in need raise a second mortgage. For the community, it may well mean an improvement in the general standard of housing. These are the good reasons why the State should give financial encouragement to owner-occupation. Arguments based on the salutary effect of owner-occupation on the character are contentious. No one will question that the greater freedom associated with owner-occupation is desirable, but the ultimate freedom is the freedom to move. This will be achieved – for householders of every tenure – only by ending the housing shortage and raising the standard of living. For the rest, even Dr Zweig has reservations about the character development of owner-occupiers:

House property also brings a man into contact with life insurance and banking. To start with, he often has to insure himself for life when engaging on a long-term mortgage. He usually gets a cheque book, since he has to pay rates, mortgage charges, insurance, and so on. He starts thinking about interest rates, local rates and local council affairs, he watches local developments in the movement of population in his neighbourhood. He wants respectable neighbours who keep their property in good order, as that affects the value of his own. Often he is not satisfied with the neighbourhood when his standard of prosperity goes up, so he moves out, in order to 'give his children a better chance'. He becomes 'respectability-minded', one could even say snobbish; he belongs to a class of his own among the working men, finding himself, as he often says, on the border of the middle classes.

He also, be it added, begins to discern the injustice of Schedule A.

In all discussion of the financial sufferings of owner-occupiers it must be remembered, not only that they are acquiring capital value, but that on a rising market they are acquiring more than they are paying for. The financial complaints of owner-occupiers are directed at their current payments – at the residue of Schedule A, or at increases in the building societies' rate of interest. Most of their financial problems derive, however, from the original necessity to find capital – for a down payment of perhaps 20 per cent of the price of a house, as well as for legal costs and the costs of moving. Many owner-occupiers have gone into debt privately in addition to obtaining mortgages. At best the need for initial capital means that wives go on working longer than they want to before having children. At worst it means the postponement of house purchase until children have grown up and are self-supporting – the Rowntree study showed that among manual workers this is not uncommon. One way of encouraging owner-occupation and easing the owner-occupier's difficulties is to increase the amount of his mortgage and to allow him until his retiring age to repay it. People might also be encouraged to start saving for a house before they actually contemplate buying one. Under a scheme operated by the Army in association with the building societies, a serving soldier can have money deducted from his pay each week for investment in a building society at $3\frac{3}{4}$ per cent. When he leaves the Army with a deposit accumulated, he is given special consideration for a building-society mortgage.

Of the current payments made by owner-occupiers, those that cause the anxiety are the unpredictable ones. The cost of redecoration and of simple repairs can be kept down to an average of a few shillings a week if the householder does the work himself, and the actual payments made at any one time – for pots of paint and the like – need not be more than a few pounds. The discovery that major repairs are needed may mean financial disaster – whether a short-term loan is raised, or the house is left to rot. The Housing Repairs and Rents Act of 1954 provided for people who had mortgages from local authorities to make regular interest-bearing deposits, to be drawn on whenever repairs had to be paid for; but little use seems to have been made of the provision. Such a practice is to be encouraged, but it cannot be relied on to provide for major repairs. Building societies insist that mortgagors take out insurance policies against fire and certain other contingencies. These policies should be made to include major repairs.

FREEHOLD, LEASEHOLD, AND HOUSING ASSOCIATIONS

In theory the leaseholder may be subject to innumerable petty restrictions. In practice action is not likely to be taken against him because his wife hangs out washing on a Tuesday, unless he is also living off her immoral earnings. But he has cause for concern in a clause which requires his house to be in good condition on the expiry of a 99-year lease. It used to be the practice for a rich man who had been unable to contain the dry rot, and whose lease was about to expire, to sell his house to a man of straw.

At present, as a result of the Landlord and Tenant Act of 1954 and of the Rent Act of 1957, a sitting tenant can normally remain in occupation on the expiry of a lease longer than twenty-one years. A landlord can claim possession only for redevelopment or in special circumstances. The lease will be regarded as unexpired unless either landlord or tenant does something about it. If a landlord and tenant fail to agree on new terms, a landlord may (and normally will) serve a notice proposing that the tenant be granted a

Rent Act statutory tenancy at a rack-rent – that is, a rent appropriate to an ordinary private tenancy, as distinct from a ground rent. The leaseholder ceases to be a leaseholder, and of course he has ceased to possess any capital value in his house. He is no longer an owner-occupier but a private tenant. The peculiar aspect of his status is that he has security of tenure even though his rent be above the limit up to which ordinary private tenants receive protection under the Rent Act.*

This is to say that the problem of leasehold tenure has been put in abeyance. It is difficult to see how it can be solved without arbitration in individual cases. The terms of future leases might be limited by legislation, to provide that on expiry the land would revert to the ground landlord but the property would still belong to the lessee. This would require the ground landlord, if he did not negotiate a new lease with the lessee (or the sale of the freehold to him), to buy the property from him. Provision could be made for arbitration in the event of failure to agree on a price. Lessees would be protected from the injustice of having to restore houses that were on their last legs, without being encouraged to neglect houses that were not. Landlords would suffer no injustice, because they would allow for their obligations to buy properties back in the prices they charged for them.

Some solution to the problem is the more desirable because leasehold property has important advantages over freehold. Where houses are grouped, a great deal of cooperation is required among freeholders, if the gardens are to be satisfactorily landscaped and cared for. The building of a communal utility room would probably not be considered practicable. Problems of cooperation largely disappear if matters in which householders have a collective interest

* This passage refers to residential tenants. Separate provisions apply to business tenants.

are the responsibility of a ground landlord. A ground landlord can also ensure that houses are painted often enough.

Cooperative housing associations afford a means of having things both ways – of combining freedom with landscaping and communal utility rooms. The traditional housing associations in this country are philanthropic organizations providing housing to let, and the legislation about housing associations is directed mainly at these. But housing cooperatives are entitled to register as housing associations. They may then apply to local authorities for 100 per cent mortgages repayable over sixty years (as against the twenty or thirty years allowed to individual owner-occupiers). Co-operatives can arrange their finances so that members get 100 per cent mortgages. Their members are of course acquiring capital value less fast than individual owner-occupiers. If a member moves after twenty or thirty years, he may take his financial share in the venture with him, but it will be a good deal less than the value of a house. What he will have gained is the occupation of a better house during those twenty or thirty years than he could otherwise have afforded.

In Scandinavia cooperatives are favoured with mortgages at extremely low interest rates. There seems, however, to be no financial reason why cooperatives should not flourish in this country under the existing arrangements. What is necessary is to reproduce the well-tried Scandinavian organizations designed to get cooperatives started, to deal with architects, contractors, and suchlike, and to keep legal fees to a minimum. The National Federation of Housing Societies will offer advice, but it has always been concerned more with associations building houses to let (as is the fund established by the 1961 Housing Act). John Greve suggests in *The Housing Problem* that housing cooperatives need their own central organization with specialists in law, finance, surveying, architecture, and housing management. The Government might subsidize such an organization, as it already does the National Federation of Housing Societies, at any rate till such time as it could be financed by subscriptions from flourishing cooperatives.

THE MONEYLENDERS

The specialists in lending money for house purchase are the building societies and the local authorities. Only they arrange for the repayment of mortgage loans by monthly instalments of capital and interest. There are about 750 building societies; and about 1,200 of the 1,500 housing authorities have used lending powers granted them under the Housing Acts and the Small Dwellings Acquisitions Acts. In 1961 the building societies lent nearly £550 million (not quite all of it to owner-occupiers) and the local authorities £99 million. The local authorities charge a higher rate of interest than the building societies (because it costs them more to borrow the money they lend). They often allow thirty years for repayment, against the building societies' twenty or twenty-five years, and they usually lend a large proportion of the purchase price – sometimes 100 per cent. Mortgage loans for the purpose of house purchase are provided by about thirty-five of the hundred-odd insurance companies: instead of making periodical repayments of capital, the borrower takes out a life-insurance policy for the amount of the mortgage, which is automatically repaid when the policy is realized. A mortgage as such – a loan on the security of a house – may be obtained from a bank or from anyone who has the money to lend.

'The aim of building society managements', declares a standard work* on housing published as late as 1957, 'is to fix the investment and mortage rates of interest so that there

* Herbert Ashworth, *Housing in Great Britain*, Thomas Skinner.

is equilibrium between the inflow of funds and the demand for mortgage accommodation.'

Today anyone who is trying to buy a house knows this is ludicrously untrue. The aim of building-society managements is to keep down the interest rates on their clients' mortgages – to keep themselves pure among contemporary usurers, to let everyone see that something more public-spirited than the profit motive determines their policies. If they hope to forestall a demand for their nationalization, they are surely misguided. The community will not indefinitely allow them to keep themselves pure at the expense of aggravating the housing problem, though to my knowledge the only journal that has criticized them so far is *The Economist*:

Moreover the rise in savings through the medium of the building societies has been less than the growth in personal savings as a whole; and mortgage business which by normal building society canons ought to be perfectly acceptable has increasingly been turned away because of lack of money to finance it. The building societies may therefore be criticized for not doing enough to satisfy their own professed aims of financing owner-occupied houses on economic terms.*

The last few years of high interest rates have merely made more manifest the inherent defect in the building societies' policy. They have always preferred not to have enough money to need to think about lending it. The rest follows from this. For a long time they would not lend money on houses that looked like council houses, and even today they will knock £500 off the amount of a mortgage for good design. For a long time they would not lend money for the purchase of flats, and even today they are reluctant to lend it for the purchase of old ones. Five years ago the conversion of large old houses into flats for sale offered one of the best

* 18 November 1961.

hopes of easing the London housing shortage quickly, and their purchase had to be financed almost entirely by mortgages from the L.C.C.

If the building societies are anxious not to inconvenience their clients with higher interest rates, they could make the normal period of repayment thirty years instead of twenty or twenty-five or, better still, allow any period up to retiring age. If they raised their interest rates by 1 per cent, they could also raise the interest they paid to investors by 1 per cent, and have a great deal more money available for lending. While lending to more people, they could increase many mortgages to 100 per cent – even, on a rising market, to 105 per cent – and so enable people to pay their legal costs and moving costs. They might lose out on an occasional deal, but they must know as well as insurance companies and *croupiers* that they do not need to win every time in order to make a profit.

The gravest responsibility that the building societies carry is for the decay of the pre-1919 houses. An estate in North London has houses now selling for £8,000 on which no building society would advance a penny, even during the acute housing shortage in the years immediately after the war. The houses in question were about a hundred years old, had been modernized, and were then selling for £2,500. They were selling only because the estate was itself able to provide mortgages for purchasers. Elsewhere houses which were no less sound structurally and no less capable of modernization are now good for nothing but demolition.

Why will the building societies not grant mortgages on pre-1919 houses, or, if they grant them at all, will grant only small ones? It is no answer to say that the risk on them is greater. The reason is that they will not do the logical thing and charge a higher rate of interest where the risk is greater. By being prepared to charge, say, an extra 2 per cent they could have granted mortgages on innumerable pre-1919 houses. Since the pre-1919 houses are for the most part the cheapest, their purchasers could have afforded the higher rates. But presumably the building societies feel it might sound bad to charge 8 per cent. Alternatively (and, given their professed aims, this is an even more reprehensible explanation) they have simply avoided having their standardized bureaucratic procedures upset by differential interest rates and the problems involved in the assessment of old houses – not but that these problems could be greatly reduced by the introduction of compulsory insurance for major repairs.

We have rather concentrated on the building societies' defects. The majority have to their credit a sound if inflexible administrative structure and an unquestioned integrity. We have already remarked that they have little truck with the profit motive. If ever the State wished to adopt a constructive national housing policy, the nationalization of the building societies would be a peculiarly painless operation. The writing was on the wall when they agreed to distribute the £100 million made available by the Government under the House Purchase and Housing Act of 1959 for the purchase of the pre-1919 houses they were allowing to rot.

STATE AID TO OWNER-OCCUPIERS

The Conservative (caretaker) Government of 1945 declared that if returned to office at the forthcoming general election it would give subsidies to purchasers of houses built by private enterprise (as well as to local authorities for council tenants). It was not returned to office, and the Labour Government gave subsidies to house purchasers only in special circumstances in rural areas. In 1945 owner-occupiers were, however, benefiting from the fact that their houses had not been revalued for income-tax purposes since before the war. Slowly this state of affairs came to be accepted; and with owner-occupiers within reach of an electoral majority, the Chancellor of the Exchequer announced in his 1962 Budget speech that Schedule A on owner-occupied houses was to be abolished: in 1963 it would be reduced prior to abolition, if it was not abolished outright.

The subsidies for council houses, which cause much indignant debate, cost the Exchequer £61 million a year. The undervaluation of owner-occupied houses, which has come about by default, costs the Exchequer well over £130 million* a year in Schedule A tax. The abolition of Schedule A on owner-occupied houses will cost a further £50 million. There are only half as many council tenants as owner-occupiers, and council tenants receive additional subsidies from the rates of £18 million. The upshot is that the average owner-occupier is already getting nearly as much financial assistance with his housing as the average council tenant, and with the abolition of his residual Schedule A tax will be getting more. What would be the political repercussions if the average council tenant knew as much about the average owner-occupier's finances as the average owner-occupier knows about his?

The council tenant's ignorance need not be attributed to conspiracy, since the owner-occupier rarely understands his own finances. It is his lack of understanding which has enabled him to demand the abolition of the residue of

* The Schedule A tax paid by owner-occupiers is about £50 million. *The Economist* (31 March 1962) calculated that the 1963 rating valuations are 3·6 times the old ones based on 1939 values. Charging Schedule A on contemporary valuations could therefore be expected to bring in another £130 million (£50 x 2·6 million) plus further amounts attributable to the facts that the present £50 million is net of allowances for repairs and decorations, and that some of the additional tax would be paid at higher rates.

Schedule A with some self-righteousness. Why, he asks, should he be taxed on income represented by his house, when he is not taxed on income represented by his other capital goods such as his cigarette lighter and his car? The explanation is that the income they represent is negligible. Matches are cheap, and petrol for a car costs about the same as train fares (which must be regarded as the alternative, since few people would hire a car for seven days a week, year in year out). Suppose, however, that someone invented an atomic car that needed no refuelling for fifty years. The Inland Revenue would immediately want to tax the income it represented – and no doubt it would have the sympathy and support of the majority of owner-occupiers who had to make do with internal combustion engines.

At the same time as the Inland Revenue introduced a tax on atomic cars it would allow the interest portion of hire-purchase payments made for them to be set against the amount assessed for tax. Self-evidently, the cost of borrowing money to buy one would reduce the income it represented. On the same principle, all the expenses associated with a house, including mortgage interest and ground rent, are chargeable as expenses against income. When the tax structure became distorted by the undervaluation of Schedule A, the amount of mortgage interest and ground rent allowable against tax should have been limited to, say, 120 per cent of Schedule A values. As it is, what are logically expenses allowable against the tax on the house are commonly four times as great as the tax itself.

Suppose that a man who earns £1,000 a year, and has two children of eight and ten, buys a leasehold house with a ground rent of £12 a year for £2,500. He would very likely get a mortgage for £2,000 at 6 per cent. For the purpose of Schedule A the net annual value of the house might be £32 a year.

			£
Salary			1,000
House			32
			1,032
less mortgage interest	120		
ground rent	12		132
			900
less earned-income relief			
(⅖ of £900)		200	
personal allowance		240	
children's allowance		200	
national insurance contributions		18	658
Tax chargeable on			242

£	s.	d.	£	s.	d.
60 at	1	9	5	5	0
150 at	4	3	31	17	6
32 at	6	3	10	0	0
			47	2	6

Suppose now that his house were given an up-to-date
Schedule A value of £115. His assessed income would go up
by £83 a year, on which he would receive earned-income
relief of £18. He would therefore pay tax on another
£65 at 6s. 3d. in the pound. This is £20 6s. 3d., or not much
less than the average subsidy for a council house. If he has
got his mortgage from a building society and is repaying
the loan in equal instalments each year, the interest on it,
and hence the amount of income-tax relief he receives,
steadily diminishes, but he continues to pay £20 6s. 3d. a
year less tax than he would with an up-to-date assessment
of the income represented by his house. Now let us consider
a 39-year-old man earning £2,000 a year who buys a freehold house for £5,000. We shall give him a wife and two
children of twelve and fourteen, and his house a net annual

value of £56 a year. His accountant explains to him that
among those who pay income tax at the standard rate only
the mugs get their mortgages from building societies. An
insurance company will give him a mortgage for £4,000
and at the same time a life-insurance policy for £4,000
realizable in twenty years' time. He will not repay the loan
in little bits, but all at once, with the £4,000 he gets when
he is sixty. His mortgage interest will remain constant
throughout the twenty years. He will get income-tax relief
not only on this, but on a proportion of the premiums for his
life-insurance policy as well. Altogether it will cost him less
than getting a mortgage from a building society, and he will
be getting life-insurance into the bargain.

		£
Salary		2,000
House		56
		2,056
less mortgage interest		240
		1,816
less earned-income relief		
(⅖ of £1,816)	404	
personal allowance	240	
children's allowance	250	
life-insurance premiums		
(⅖ of £170 13s. 4d.)	68	
national insurance contributions	18	980
Tax chargeable on		836

£	s. d.	£ s. d.
60	at 1 9	5 5 0
150	at 4 3	31 17 6
150	at 6 3	46 17 6
476	at 7 9	184 9 0
		268 9 0

If his house had an up-to-date Schedule A value of £202, his income would be £146 a year higher. On this he would be allowed earned-income relief of £32. He would therefore pay tax at 7s. 9d. in the pound on another £114. This is £44 3s. 6d. Furthermore, if he had not been earning a high income, he would not have been able to save money by taking out a life-insurance policy. It is possible he would have wanted life-insurance anyway, but with no life-insurance he would have had to pay tax at 7s. 9d. in the pound on a further £68. This is £26 7s. The total increase in his income tax would have been £70 10s. 6d.

This then is the working of the present State aid to owner-occupiers. The man earning £500 a year and struggling to buy a house gets no aid at all. He does not pay income tax; nor would he do so if Schedule A were based on up-to-date values. The man earning £1,000 a year and buying a house comparable to a council house gets nearly as much aid as a council tenant. The man earning £2,000 a year and buying a house twice as desirable as a council house gets nearly twice as much aid as a council tenant if he believes in life-insurance and nearly three times as much if he does not. In addition, if he does not believe in life-insurance he gets it given to him. And the owner-occupier millionaire with a town house and a country mansion gets more aid with his housing than old-age pensioners have to live on.

The abolition of the residue of Schedule A will give our £1,000-a-year man another £7 6s. 3d. a year and our £2,000-a-year man another £16 13s. 3d. It will leave the £500-a-year owner-occupier without any aid. It will give the owner-occupier millionaire another old-age pension. People will be even further encouraged to buy second houses for themselves. We may expect to see even more expensive new flats that would normally have been let being sold leasehold with ground rents comparable to rack-rents. If the Government is determined to spend £200 million a year on owner-occupiers, it could at least find a better way of doing it.

New valuations will be brought into force for rating purposes in 1963. The Chancellor could announce that they will be brought into force for Schedule A as well, but that he will simultaneously introduce a new scheme for aiding owner-occupiers. If he does not wish to appear less generous than his promise, he could even declare that the entire proceeds of Schedule A will be redistributed among owner-occupiers, but with something going to the £500-a-year man and nothing going to the millionaire. Since there are many more £500-a-year men than millionaires, the Conservatives could expect to gain even more votes (to set off, perhaps, against diminished funds).

In January 1962 Birmingham Corporation sold 108 houses and provided nearly 100 per cent mortgages on them at only 4½ per cent interest. Differential interest rates are one means by which the State might help the less well-off owner-occupier. Whereas income-tax reliefs help the £500-a-year man not at all, a reduction of 1 per cent in the interest on a £1,000 mortgage would save him 3s. 10d. a week. A reduction of 1 per cent in the £1,000-a-year man's interest on a £2,000 mortgage would save him 5s. 3d. a week – less than twice as much, because he would forgo relief on income tax at 6s. 3d. in the pound. As a short-term policy for the encouragement of owner-occupation, the provision of mortgages at low interest rates to those with incomes below a certain amount would have been far superior to the undervaluation or abolition of Schedule A. As a long-term policy, something more equitable still is required. In the last chapter we shall consider how the State might provide appropriate aid to all householders regardless of their tenure.

D

5 Private Tenancy

BEFORE the First World War, nine-tenths of all houses were privately rented. Owning one's own house was on the whole a privilege of the well-to-do. Council housing was practically unheard of. Today there are between 4 and 4½ million privately rented unfurnished dwellings and a few hundred thousand furnished ones. Together they constitute less than a third of the dwellings in England and Wales. The Rent Act, so far from reviving private tenancy, has about doubled the rate at which privately rented houses are transferred to owner-occupation. A hundred thousand or more privately rented houses a year are now bought for owner-occupation, half of them by sitting tenants. Another 60,000 a year are compulsorily purchased by local authorities for demolition in slum-clearance programmes. Others are demolished in the course of development schemes. Moreover, if we set about urban renewal in earnest, we should substitute a figure of 200,000 a year for the 60,000 of the present slum-clearance programme. Examining the trends, one could almost wonder why the Labour Party's earlier intention to municipalize privately rented property caused any fuss.

The Rowntree study showed that over half of the households in privately rented (unfurnished) property in England have no fixed bath of their own. Five per cent have no kitchen sink, 8 per cent no flush lavatory, and 53 per cent no hot-water supply. Not even the combination of the Rent Act and improvement grants is doing much to reduce these proportions. About 26,000 baths a year are being installed in private property. At this rate it will take a century and a quarter to equip the more than 3 million privately rented houses that now have either no bath or a shared one. Those in the north are in the greatest need of repair and improvement. In the big cities private rents are twice as much as in the rural districts and small towns. Since the rents of council houses do not differ greatly from town to country, the private tenant in a big city can usually move to a council house without much change in rent, while the rural private tenant who moves to a council house must expect his rent to double.

Private tenants include higher proportions of old people, young people, and single people. They also, of course, include higher proportions of the unsettled and the itinerant. Every social class is represented among them, but if nothing is done to reverse the trends, the middle income groups will increasingly desert to council tenancy and owner-occupation. The long-term private tenants are unskilled manual workers, old-age pensioners, and the very rich.

The reason there are not more moderately rich tenants is that the moderately rich choose not to pay rent out of taxed income. Instead of renting a flat, a man will nowadays buy one leasehold, paying a small price for it and a large ground rent. On the ground rent he obtains income-tax relief. The gain consists in the fact that he pays tax on less than the true Schedule A value of his house, whereas if he were a tenant his landlord would pay tax on a rent representing the true value of the house. The abolition of Schedule A will destroy any hope of reviving private tenancy even in expensive property. As it is, the rich tenant tends, unless his firm pays his rent, to be very rich – a man who will pay a great deal for mobility and legal simplicity.

Private tenants are the only householders who receive no

financial aid from the State (except in so far as they benefit from improvement grants claimed by landlords). The State's contribution to their well-being has consisted in rent control, which is to say that it has claimed financial aid for them from their landlords. Apart from being hard on landlords, this has meant that in return for low rents private tenants have had to accept low housing standards. Rent control is now in the process of being abolished. It cannot, however, be expected that private tenancy will thereafter revive in competition with two other forms of tenure which are subsidized by the State. In theory a private tenant's main anxiety should be his insecurity of tenure – the possibility of eviction or of an increase in rent. Sometimes indeed it is. But few tenants sought to take advantage of the clause in the Rent Act whereby they could get three years' security of tenure if they negotiated an increase in their rents within a year. Innumerable tenants who could legally be evicted at a month's notice have absolute confidence in their landlords' goodwill or inertia. Their anxieties are whether their houses are going to fall down or whether they will be able to save up enough to install the amenities the landlord will not pay for – or, while they are about it, to save up enough for down payments on houses of their own. There are indeed tenants who have asked their landlords not to repair or improve their houses. Because they are saving up to buy their own houses, they want to keep their rents as low as possible.

THE RENT ACT

Rent control is a lingering war-time expedient. When the Second World War broke out there were some four million houses that had been controlled since the First World War. The Rent and Mortgage Restrictions Act of 1939 forbade increases in the rent of houses with rateable values not exceeding £100 in the Metropolitan Police District and not exceeding £75 elsewhere in England and Wales. Less than 100,000 privately rented houses in England and Wales remained free of control – until new building was resumed after the war, when, as between the wars, a new house could be let for an unlimited rent. The Landlord and Tenant (Rent Control) Act of 1949 did empower the rent tribunals, established to determine the rents of furnished houses, to determine also the rents of new houses, but, in general, whether or not houses have been controlled has depended on when they were built.

Whenever a house was brought under control it could be assumed that the existing rent represented its value. Ten or twenty years on, its value would depend on the repairs that had been carried out. The Housing Act of 1949 empowered local authorities to grant and lend money to landlords for improvements and conversions, but the local authorities were as reluctant to provide the money (and to divert building capacity from their own programmes) as the landlords were to claim it. The first tentative step towards decontrol was taken by the Housing Repairs and Rents Act of 1954, which allowed landlords to increase rents if they could show that they had spent money to keep their houses in a good state of repair.

The Rent Act of 1957 for the first time related control to value. It abolished control on dwellings with rateable values of more than £40 in Greater London and more than £30 elsewhere in England and Wales and permitted increases in the rents of houses remaining under control according to their gross values (as well as to their landlords' responsibility for maintaining them). It also removed control from all houses let to new tenants. The difficulty of assessing the effects of the Rent Act may be illustrated by a quotation from the official report of inquiry:

In one of our questions we dealt with those people who had received notice to quit under the Rent Act and who were still there. Clearly we knew nothing of those who had received notice and had already left by April 1959.*

This much is certain, that the effects of the Rent Act were not what either the Government or the Opposition foretold. The Government did not even know how many houses it was decontrolling. It appears to have identified rateable properties with households or dwellings. Many rateable properties accommodate a number of separate tenancies, representing only a portion of the rateable value of the whole. Only 317,000 dwellings were decontrolled by virtue of their rateable values, against the 750,000 predicted. Scarcely less surprising (though here the Government made no prediction) is the fact that as many as 320,000 houses a year are becoming decontrolled as a result of the voluntary movement (or deaths) of their tenants.

The Rowntree study showed that, two years after the Rent Act, rents (exclusive of rates and service charges) were clustering at twice gross value in controlled houses and three times in decontrolled. They were still on average lower than council rents, but gross value for gross value they were higher. The range around the average was remarkable. Nearly half a million houses were let at rents below their (1939) gross values. More than half a million were let at illegally high rents. In general, rents appeared to bear no relation to landlords' responsibility for repairs. Even with years of neglect to be made up for, privately rented houses were being repaired no more frequently than owner-occupied and council houses. Many of the repairs were being paid for by the tenants. Where improvements (as distinct from repairs) were being made, they were usually being paid for by the tenants.

* *Rent Act 1957: Report of Inquiry*, H.M.S.O., Cmnd 1246, 1960.

The Rowntree study found no evidence that the Rent Act had reduced 'under-occupation'. It seems clear that comparatively few tenants have been either evicted or driven from their homes by increased rents as a result of the Act. People have moved out of controlled houses in some numbers, but for the most part voluntarily. We have already remarked that there is a steady movement out of privately-rented houses and into better houses. But, if the Rent Act ended in anticlimax, it must not be inferred that rent control is unimportant. The houses still controlled – and they are the vast majority of privately rented houses – are the least valuable. By and large they contain the least well-off tenants. They also, by definition, contain tenants who have chosen not to abandon the privilege of rent control by moving. (Indeed, the Rent Act will have deterred from moving some people who before the Act would have gone from one rent-controlled house to another.) The next measure of decontrol is liable to cause more hardship. What we should do, of course, is to abolish rent control and simultaneously begin giving State aid to private tenants on rational principles.

LANDLORDS

When it was proposing to municipalize privately-rented property, the Labour Party did its best to present landlords as grinding the faces of the poor. Since control had kept private rents absurdly low – much lower than the rents of council houses – criticism had to be concentrated on the poor state of privately-rented property. To this day few Left-wing writers can conceive of private landlords as other than evil. In *The Housing Problem*, John Greve declares: 'It is one of the myths of housing that rented houses are in their present state because of rent control.' As evidence of this, he cites the fact that comparatively few privately-rented houses had bathrooms, lavatories, or hot-water systems even before rent control was introduced. Before rent control was introduced – in 1915 – these amenities were of course comparative luxuries, and their installation by landlords would have required rents beyond the means of most of the working class. John Greve even carries his argument to its logical conclusion:

The major deficiencies in privately-rented houses have not developed since 1939 under the régime of rent control; they date from before the Kaiser's war, and a large proportion of them from before the Boer War – or even the Crimean War.

He also argues that between the wars even controlled rents were high enough to allow for repairs. This is probably true, but it surely has to be allowed that the existence and unpredictability of rent control were a considerable deterrent to investment in private housing.

The authors of the interim Rowntree study go to the other extreme. All the Government's assumptions about the effects of the Rent Act, they say, followed from its premise that landlords would behave like 'economic men': in the event, they have not done so. In an article in the *Guardian*, Professor Donnison went so far as to write: 'If the level of rents is now effectively limited by social and economic factors, argument about further decontrol may be largely irrelevant.'* Economic men, however, can display social responsibility or experience social embarrassment without actually undergoing a change of personality. The Rowntree study itself showed that landlords were less inhibited about charging economic rents to new tenants in decontrolled property than to existing tenants, and the official inquiry into the effects of the Rent Act gave further evidence of this. It must be remembered, too, that existing tenants could appeal to the courts against extortionate rents, and that

* D. V. Donnison, *Manchester Guardian*, 10 July 1959.

landlords had a vested interest in limiting the unpopularity of decontrol. Their failure to seize their chance to charge higher rents by improving their properties is in no way incompatible with their role as economic men. Most of them must be right in believing that on financial grounds their properties do not justify further investment. In the 1961 Housing Act the Government has increased the permitted return on expenditure on improvement from 8 per cent to 12½ per cent. Landlords can still decline to be drawn without jeopardizing their reputations for business acumen.

The truth is that even before rent control was introduced investment in housing for rent had begun to fall, and that today it offers no scope to economic men. One of the effects of rent control was to keep trapped in housing a lot of capital which would otherwise have been withdrawn. The speed with which landlords of decontrolled properties are selling them for owner-occupation is evidence of this, as also is the failure of private enterprise to build new low-cost housing for rent.

What is regarded as the best evidence that landlords are not economic men comes from J. B. Cullingworth's study of landlords in Lancaster:

There are at present 853 private landlords in Lancaster. In total they own 2,631 houses. Well over half of them own only one house. A third of them are seventy or more years old, and a further quarter are aged between sixty and seventy. Their average weekly income (including net income from rents) is less than £10 a week. Nearly three-quarters of them obtained their dwellings by inheritance. Very few have sufficient capital to improve their houses even if they were inclined to do so. But, in fact, to most their houses are a responsibility which they intend to shed at the earliest opportunity.

Comparison with 1948 (for which year local records have been analysed) shows that over nine hundred landlords have gone out of business in the past twelve years – most by selling to owner-occupiers.

The question which J. B. Cullingworth poses about the character of private landlords seems to me to contain false alternatives. 'Are they', he writes, '"economic men", owning large numbers of houses and seeking to maximize their profits – or are they elderly widows owning one or two houses and incapable of formulating any rational policy for their management?' On his own evidence, they appear to be elderly widows capable of formulating the entirely rational policy of maximizing their profits by selling their houses and investing the proceeds in gilt-edged. Both his own study and the Rowntree study provide information not so much about landlords as about the state of the market in rented housing. In introducing both improvement grants and the Rent Act, the Government certainly made false assumptions, but the main one was about the state of the market.

The same false assumption lies behind the Government's attempts to encourage the building of new housing for rent. Under the 1961 Housing Act it has established a £25 million fund from which loans are made to approved non-profit-making housing associations which are prepared to build houses and let them at cost rent. It regards this as 'essentially a pump-priming operation' and hopes that 'it will serve to show the way to the investment of private capital once again in building houses to let.'*

If private enterprise is to build houses for rent, it must be able to make a profit out of them, and it must have an assurance (as distinct from a promise) that they will not in the future be made subject to rent control. At present they cannot even make a profit. We have remarked that investment in houses for rent had begun to decline before rent control was introduced. Since then rigorous housing standards have been laid down. In addition, council housing has been invented and owner-occupation has become feasible for the lower income groups. Most important of all, both council

* 1961 White Paper.

housing and owner-occupation are subsidized. It is unfair competition.

The Government is no doubt right if it believes that part of the reluctance of tenants to pay economic rents is attributable to conditioning to low rents by rent control (and by subsidies for council houses). In return for good housing, people can certainly be persuaded to pay more rent than they have been accustomed to. Many indeed will need no persuading. Households with incomes of from £10 to £14 a week already spend an average of a fifth of their incomes on housing. One can assume that there are larger numbers of people who would pay between £3 10s. and £4 a week. Unfortunately this is not quite an economic rent.

If a development company is to build houses for rent, manage them, and allow something for depreciation, it must have at least a 10 per cent return on its investment. It cannot erect family flats, let alone actual houses, for less than £2,250 to £3,000 (according to the cost of the land), which puts minimum economic rents at more than £4 a week. Minimum economic rents for actual houses must be between £5 and £6 a week. That there is difficulty in finding enough tenants to pay these rents is of course all the more reason why rented housing ought to be provided. People who cannot afford to rent new houses can even less afford to buy them. Unless, therefore, local authorities are to provide a vastly increased amount of rented housing, which many of them do not even want to do, the State must subsidize private rented housing.

Subsidies of the kind now given to local authorities are both inequitable and wasteful. In any case, private enterprise would be reluctant to accept them. The local authorities would inevitably want a say in the selection of tenants. And, while there could be confidence that subsidies granted for particular houses would never be withdrawn, the practice of granting subsidies to private enterprise might always be stopped, which is to say that organizations and building plans based on them would always be vulnerable.

The solution is for the State to give individual householders aid with their housing, according to their incomes and dependants, and to let them spend it how they will – on renting a council house or a private house, or on buying a house. Where they spent it on houses built by private enterprise, whether to buy them or rent them, the State would have to make its own valuation of their worth (or there would be infinite scope for corruption). The valuations for rating purposes could normally be used; but, as we have seen, rateable properties are not synonymous with separate dwellings; and new houses would have to be valued before tenants moved in. Just as the building societies' valuations, which determine the amounts of mortgages, already exercise some restraint on the prices of houses sold to owner-occupiers, so valuations determining financial aid for tenants would exercise some restraint on rents. A tenant would be free to pay a higher rent than the amount on which his State aid was based, as an owner-occupier can pay a purchase price above the building society's valuation. But prospective tenants would benefit, as prospective owner-occupiers do, from the existence of objective valuations.

Once a scheme of this kind had been introduced it would be most unlikely to be withdrawn, because it could not be withdrawn without upsetting the finances of the majority of the electorate. It would provide a source of finance on which private enterprise could rely and it would carry no administrative interference with it. Widespread urban renewal would then become a proposition. Cooperation between private developers and local authorities would be necessary only to secure the compulsory purchase of old properties and arrange for the rehousing of their tenants.

The worst thing that landlords do as a class is to discriminate in their choice of tenants. So far as small landlords are concerned, discrimination may not take the form of deciding never to have a black family, or any family with children, as tenants: it may simply be the result of always choosing the most desirable tenants from a number of applicants (and of course the greater the housing shortage the greater the number of applicants). If the Labour Party had wanted a good argument for municipalization, it lay to hand in the need to ensure that houses went to tenants in the greatest need. Municipalization would not have prevented the problem of the homeless, but it could have ensured that fewer of the homeless were families with young children. Municipalization was, however, a nonstarter. As we shall see in the next chapter, the local authorities' housing administrations are inadequate to contend with the existing council houses, let alone with four million dilapidated private houses as well. The landlords of large housing estates are not in fact likely to discriminate against families with young children, but they might discriminate against coloured families or some other group. It would be a good idea to provide that where landlords possessing more than a certain number of houses have tenants who are receiving State aid with their rent, they should be obliged to let a proportion of their houses to families with children and a proportion to coloured families. It could be left to local authorities to enforce the provision where it was appropriate to do so. Private enterprise should be prepared to put up with this much administrative interference in return for an acceptable form of subsidy. The provision would in any case steadily diminish in importance as the shortage of good housing was overcome.

6 Council Tenancy

THE $3\frac{1}{2}$ million council tenants conform closely to the indignant Conservative's image of them. While they include professional men and business men at one extreme, and the very poor (particularly among the old) at the other, they are for the most part manual workers capable of paying more than the subsidized rent – at least in the sense in which owner-occupiers could pay more than the reduced Schedule A tax. Even when their rents are not subsidized, council tenants can be regarded as fortunate in having the houses they have for what they pay for them. Not all council houses are new, but nearly all are in good repair and have a lavatory, a bath, and the usual kitchen equipment. (Strictly defined, council houses include slums bought to be abolished.)

The difficulty is in becoming a council tenant. The man who set about it efficiently would get an essential job, marry young, father a child a year, find himself a slum flat, share it with another family, and develop chronic ill-health. With all these qualifications he could even expect to get a house before he was thirty. In addition to the price he paid in inconvenience (and indeed in the expense of a large family), he would have to resign himself to immobility before as well as after he got his house: despite repeated pleas from the Government, the local authority is likely to require several years' residence in the district before it will put him on its waiting list. With the reduction in local authorities' building programmes which followed the abolition of the general-

needs subsidy in 1956, many waiting lists were closed.
Under the 1961 Housing Act, houses for general needs are
again subsidized, but there will not be as many built as
before 1956.

Council housing has failed as a means of providing for the
poorest. That a local authority cannot afford the rent re-
bates necessary to provide houses for all those who want
them is not apparent if it does not have the houses anyway.
So long as a local authority has a long waiting list, there
may be a feeling that everyone's turn will come eventually.
In the rural districts there is no illusion. The rural authorities are generally worse off than the urban, not only because
their ratepayers and tenants are worse off, but because they
have fewer pre-war houses on which they are drawing subsidies. The slums apart, housing standards are generally
lower in the country than in the town, yet there are rural
authorities which cannot find tenants for houses they have
already built. A potential owner-occupier who inquires
about an improvement grant for an old house may be
offered a tenancy in a council house instead – when the
house he would have bought is left to rot.

The virtue of the council houses is that they have mostly
gone to families with growing children. Today three out of
five council tenants have children under sixteen, which is to
say both that they greatly need their houses and that they
use them fully. Ten years on, we may see many subsidized
council houses with two or three earners in them. Twenty
years on we may see many with the parents living alone in
them. Local authorities will need to build a great many
more one-bedroomed flats if the parents are not to stay put
and so re-create the post-war housing shortage for the next
generation. If the parents are reluctant to be enticed into
small flats, they should certainly be charged an unsubsidized
rent for their houses. The local authorities would also be
well-advised to turn their attention to houses with movable

partitions between the rooms. Such houses can be adapted to the changing needs of a growing family, and can finally be subdivided. The Ministry's research and development group is already studying their possibilities.

A council tenant living in a house he likes has very few problems. As one of Dr Zweig's affluent workers put it: 'You have it for life, it's like your own, cheaper, nothing to worry about, when out of work you get consideration, no responsibility anyhow.' A serious problem will arise for a council tenant only if he wants to move. But not only will he have had to wait a long time to get into his house; even when he is in it, he may not like it. The disadvantage of council tenancy is lack of choice. (That this lack of choice has been responsible for some of the best as well as some of the worst architecture in the country we must conscientiously regard as beside the point.) Whereas private tenants and owner-occupiers decide what they can afford to pay and then look for the best they can get for it, the council tenant puts his name on a waiting list and takes the first house – or if he greatly dislikes the look of this one and has a very strong will – the second house he is offered. He has probably never sat down to decide how much he is willing to spend on housing. The only question he is likely to have asked himself is whether he can afford the rent the local authority asks. He may not even be aware of the extent to which this rent is subsidized.

Since local authorities virtually decide who shall be their tenants, and since their tenants could find equivalent houses for themselves only at a far greater cost, the usual balance of power between landlord and tenant scarcely exists. Local authorities, like nearly all organizations undertaking activities other than for financial gain, do have a propensity to think they know what is good for people, and as things stand they are able to indulge it. A local authority will equip its houses with dustbins, in order to ensure that every tenant has one and does not defile his backyard with rubbish bursting out of cardboard boxes. The time comes when a tenant decides that his dustbin has had its day and needs replacing. A local-authority representative inspects it, and, mindful of a current credit squeeze, decides that it is good for another twelve months. If the tenant is sufficiently irked to go out and buy a new dustbin for himself, he is liable to be told that it is the wrong size and shape and must be removed.

Problems of this kind arise also between private tenants and landlords and between owner-occupiers and ground landlords. Moreover, the usual balance of power between landlord and tenant is everywhere upset by the condition of housing shortage. But the problems are much more acute in council tenancy. It is not only that the council tenant is even less free to move than the private tenant. The private tenant can at least hate his landlord for taking advantage of the conditions of shortage for his own financial gain. The council tenant knows that he is fortunate in having his house, and feels he has been done a favour. The local authority which is his landlord never does anything for its own financial gain. It always acts in its wisdom for its tenants' own advantage. In the long run, power employed paternalistically provokes far greater resentment than power employed selfishly or even antagonistically. Because there is no satisfactory outlet for it, the resentment accumulates.

Excuses can be made for the local authorities' paternalism. They have to fulfil their role as landlords, without being able to resort to the ultimate sanction of the private landlord, which is eviction. A local authority can evict a tenant from a particular house, but the tenant and his family, being then homeless, remain its responsibility. Problem families of all kinds become the responsibility of the local authority's welfare services, regardless of whether they are council tenants or not. Even so, there can be no

justification for such paternalist antics as evicting a family for
an hour – that is, humiliating it by stacking its furniture in the
front garden – as a warning to other bad payers. Local
authorities usually possess some undesirable houses that
they can threaten to move people to. They also have resort
to the courts for the collection of debts.

It is often said of industrial strikes over wages that their
real cause is repressed resentment deriving from day-to-day
industrial relations. Similarly the rent strikes that followed
the introduction of differential rent schemes must have
given release to repressed resentment deriving from land-
lord-tenant relations. The protests against a means test
were not merely rationalizations of a reluctance to pay
higher rents. Differential rent schemes were resented because they foisted on the local authorities the ultimate
paternalist responsibility of deciding how much pocket
money their tenants should be allowed to keep. Local authorities deserve sympathy for their reluctance to exercise this
responsibility. It is as imperative that they should be relieved
of it as that council tenants who can afford to should pay
economic rents. The council tenant who needs financial
assistance should receive it through some other organ of the
State, established to assist private tenants and owner-occupiers as well. He could then claim his assistance without loss
of dignity, and he would always pay his full rent to his landlord. Equally his landlord would always be entitled to claim
it from him.

SUBSIDIES

The rents paid by council tenants cover less than three-
quarters of the cost of their houses. Those paid by council
tenants in the metropolitan boroughs (in London County)
cover little more than half. In 1959–60 the Government
subsidies cost £60 million and contributions from the rates

£18 million. Whether or not contributions are made from the rates is now a policy decision for each local authority. They are more often made in urban than in rural districts. Among the urban authorities, rate contributions are made by all those in London County, by most of those in the north-western region, and by less than half of those in the northern and south-eastern regions. It is impossible to assemble up-to-date figures of rents and subsidies for all council houses. The following analysis* of the 1960–1 housing revenue accounts of the large majority of housing authorities which sent returns to the Institute of Municipal Treasurers and Accountants, gives a good idea of the extent to which the cost of council housing is apportioned by the different kinds of authorities between tenants, ratepayers, and taxpayers:

	County boroughs %	Metropolitan boroughs and City of London %	London County Council %	Non-county boroughs %	Urban districts %	Rural districts %
Rents	70·1	53·8	70·4	73·3	72·5	73·2
Exchequer subsidy	21·1	26·9	20·2	20·8	22·3	23·5
Rate subsidy	8·0	18·5	8·8	5·2	4·4	2·6
Other income	0·8	0·8	0·6	0·7	0·8	0·7
	100·0	100·0	100·0	100·0	100·0	100·0

* From *Housing Statistics (England and Wales) 1960–61*, Institute of Municipal Treasurers and Accountants.

The variations in rents were remarkable. For a post-war three-bedroomed house, average rents in the different county boroughs varied from 15s. 9d. a week (Manchester) to £2 0s. 4d. (Croydon); in the different metropolitan boroughs from £1 4s. 9d. (Stepney) to £3 (Hampstead); in the non-county boroughs from 15s. 2d. (Batley) to £2 11s. 9d. (Finchley); in the urban districts from 14s. 11d. (Denholme) to £2 3s. 7d. (East Barnet); in the rural districts from 15s. 9d. (Nidderdale) to £1 18s. 8d. (Petersfield). (The L.C.C.'s average was £1 10s. 3d.)

The variations in rents charged by individual local authorities depended partly on whether they possessed pre-war houses but largely on whether differential rent schemes had been adopted: the range round Manchester's average of 15s. 9d. was only from 13s. 9d. to 16s. 3d.; that round Croydon's average of £2 0s. 4d. was from 18s. 8d. to £2 11s. The range round Denholme's average of 14s. 11d. was only from 14s. 6d. to 15s. 5d.; that round East Barnet's average of £2 3s. 7d. was from 12s. 9d. to £2 5s. 6d. Nidderdale's 'average' of 15s. 9d. was in fact an invariable rent. So too was Hampstead's 'average' of £3 – but a differential rent scheme has since been introduced. The highest rent of all was in the City: £5 8s. 3d. a week. The lowest of all was in Leeds: 6d. a week. (In Scotland very low rents are common. It was only recently, after considerable coercion, that Dunbartonshire raised the rent of a three-bedroomed house from 2s. 10d. a week to 7s. 5d.)

During the thirties subsidies were given only for the rehousing of the slum-cleared. The Housing (Temporary Provisions) Act of 1944 provided for their extension to houses built for general needs. Building costs had risen since 1939, and it was clear that without subsidies local authorities would not be able to provide houses at rents which the lower-income groups could afford. In 1946 the Exchequer subsidy was fixed at £16 10s. a year for sixty years, and it was provided that there should be a rate subsidy of £5 10s. a year throughout this period. There were additional special subsidies including a discretionary subsidy for the very poor authorities.

Subsidies were greatest when the Conservatives were fulfilling their promise to build 300,000 houses a year – and their higher interest rates had increased the cost of the local authorities' borrowing. From 1952 to 1955 the Exchequer subsidy was £26 14s. and the rate subsidy £8 18s. By 1955 total subsidies amounted to over £90 million a year, and it was estimated that they were increasing by £10 million a year. The general-needs subsidy was first reduced and then, in 1956, abolished. At the same time local authorities were relieved of the obligation to provide a subsidy from the rates. From 1956 to 1961 Exchequer subsidies were restricted to certain kinds of housing: £10 a year for one-bedroomed dwellings (intended for the old); £22 1s. for houses built in connexion with slum clearance; £24 a year for houses built in the New Towns or in the overspill areas. At the time of the 1961 Housing Act, the maximum discretionary subsidy for the very poor authorities was £30 a house; there was an additional semi-recoverable subsidy for overspill of £8, and a £24 subsidy for houses needed urgently for incoming industrial workers; there were also subsidies for high blocks of flats, expensive sites, certain agricultural dwellings, protection against subsidence, and the use of special materials (for example, local stone in the Cotswolds and the Lake District).

The 1961 White Paper made two important points: that the existing system did not provide adequate assistance for the poorer local authorities; that it was not flexible enough to meet the individual needs of authorities in general. Embodying the proposals of the White Paper, the 1961 Housing Act abolished the special subsidies for slum clearance and one-bedroomed houses, and substituted a new general-needs subsidy for all housing which the Minister

could be satisfied was necessary. (It was intended to be
different from the pre-1956 general-needs subsidy. As a
rule the Minister cannot be satisfied that general-needs
housing is necessary today.) The act provided, for the first
time, for differential subsidies. Poorer authorities can claim
a subsidy of £24 a house, richer ones only £8 a house.
Authorities qualify for the higher subsidy if their expenditure on housing is greater than an assumed income of
twice the gross value for rating purposes* of all their
houses. There is special provision for authorities that just
fail to qualify for the higher subsidy. Expenditure is judged
against an assumed income instead of against actual income,
so that authorities shall not qualify by virtue of charging
low rents or of making no contribution from the rates. The
1961 Act also raised the maximum discretionary subsidy
from £30 a house to £40, the basic 'overspill' subsidy
from £24 to £28, and the additional semi-recoverable
'overspill' subsidy from £8 to £12. The other special subsidies remain in being, with modifications. The total cost of
the Exchequer subsidies – £61 million a year, increasing by
£3 million a year – was not expected to be changed by the Act.

The 1961 Act received a poor press, which seems unjusti-
fied. It restores to the local authorities some degree of autonomy in deciding for what purposes to build (though they
remain committed to their slum-clearance programmes).
At the same time it makes a serious attempt to give the most
assistance where it is most needed. Its unenthusiastic recep-
tion may have been due partly to its complexity, but was
probably due mainly to the fact that, in making minor
reforms, it drew attention to how much was wrong. That
Bournemouth qualifies for the £24 subsidy and Liverpool
for the £8 subsidy† suggests that strictly financial principles,

* As determined by the 1956 valuation based on 1939 values.

† See Raphael Samuel, James Kincaid, Elizabeth Slater, 'But Nothing Happens', *New Left Review*, January–April 1962.

however well thought out, will never effect equitable discrimination.

Apart from subsidies, building costs, and the cost of land, the variables in local-authority housing finance are rent, rates, and the cost of borrowing capital. Not only do the poorer authorities have by definition the poorer tenants and poorer ratepayers, but they have been more affected than the richer authorities by the Government's policy on local-authority borrowing. Since 1955 local authorities have been requested wherever possible to raise money on the open market, instead of (as during the early post-war years) from the Public Works Loan Board. The cost of borrowing capital includes not only the present high interest rates, but the overheads associated with public issues or mortgages. The most we can hope for, under the present administrative and financial structure, is that the differentials in the subsidies given to the poorer and richer authorities will from time to time be increased. Even if it wished to, the Ministry could not discriminate accurately between the needs of the 1,469 different housing authorities.

REGIONAL AUTHORITIES

During the early post-war housing drive it no doubt seemed both to private builders and to would-be householders that the local authorities had been given absolute power over them. It did not seem so to the local authorities themselves. As Professor Donnison has put it: 'The local authorities played the part of company commanders and battalion commanders in this campaign – and were in some respects as omnipotent and in others as impotent as the metaphor implies.'* Ministerial approval was needed for every step of every housing project – for the selection of a site, the

* *Housing Policy since the War*, Codicote Press, Welwyn, 1960.

layout of a site, the plans of individual homes to be built on a site, advertisement for tenders, and acceptance of a tender.

This strict control was made inevitable by the local authorities' lack of qualified people – and by the Labour Government's decision not to offend them by introducing new regional authorities. That local authorities became more autonomous during the 1950s was due less to the relaxation of the housing drive than to the growing number of surveyors, architects, and accountants on local authorities' staffs. The Ministry encouraged the trend, by indicating that site layouts and house designs were more likely to be approved – and approved quickly – if prepared by qualified people. New forms were provided in which the responsible officer could insert his qualifications. All this needs to be said, because it is not generally realized how ill-equipped the country was to tackle housing as a social service when the Welfare State was introduced. Finding extra teachers to cope with the expansion of education was in comparison a simple problem. At least everyone knew what teachers were. To this day the qualifications for housing administrators and planners are not standardized.

The actual administration of housing and planning is scarcely standardized at all. An inquiry made a few years ago by the housing management sub-committee of the Central Housing Advisory Committee found that of fifty-seven authorities, twenty-seven had a housing manager in charge of a separate housing department, eleven had a housing manager in charge of a section within another officer's department, eight had a housing manager with no separate department or section, and eleven had no housing manager. The work of housing administration is performed variously by the clerk's department, the treasurer's department, and the planning department. Similarly, the work of planning is performed variously by the clerk's department, the borough engineer's department, the architect's department, and the planning department. Since the housing problems of local authorities vary greatly, it is not desirable that their administrative structures should be identical. None the less, it is clear that many of the existing structures are inadequate, unduly idiosyncratic, or both. The division of planning responsibilities between the borough engineer's department and the architect's department was one of the reasons for Mr R. B. Connell's resignation as chief planning assistant of Worthing in February 1962. At the other extreme are the many authorities where both planning and architecture are the responsibility of the borough engineer's department, which may contain no architect.

If the country already had enough good houses in the right places, and housing administration were confined to rent collection, repairs, and the arrangement of transfers, then the local authorities could be left to get on with it, with the occasional guidance that they now get from the Minister and his Advisory Committee. Their present responsibilities for extensive new building, slum clearance, redevelopment, and rehousing (including the rehousing of overspill population outside their borders) are clearly too much for them, and would remain so even with administrative reform.

With the exception of the L.C.C., the housing authorities form the lowest tier of local government above parish councils. The L.C.C. is the only county council which is a housing authority, and it became one fortuitously, by inheriting powers from the old Metropolitan Board of Works. (Both the L.C.C. and the metropolitan boroughs are housing authorities. They hold concurrent powers.) The architecturally famous blocks of flats which have replaced many of London's slums are the result of an administrative fluke. The benefits that have derived from the L.C.C.'s use of its powers were succinctly stated by the Ministry in its evidence to the Royal Commission on Local Government in Greater London:

The large numbers of houses built by the L.C.C. both inside and outside the County have made it possible for population to be redistributed so as to help to relieve overcrowding in the worst congested areas of the County. But for this help, a number of boroughs would have had to rehouse families at undesirably high densities.

The wide geographical distribution of the houses owned by the L.C.C. has enabled the Council to do something to bring about a closer correlation between workplace and residence, thus helping to reduce length and strain of the journey to work.

The financial resources of the County as a whole have been made available to help reduce the burden of cost falling on the boroughs, particularly the poorer ones with the biggest slum clearance problems. *

Add to these considerations that (apart from the L.C.C.) only certain consortia of local authorities have been able to afford research and development into architectural problems, and the case for housing authorities covering everywhere much wider areas than the boroughs and district councils is complete. Nowadays the case for regional authorities as such is widely accepted, but it is sometimes allowed to rest on the needs of town and country planning. Certainly the counties and county boroughs cannot fulfil their responsibilities as the supreme planning authorities. The English counties were not created to aid administration but to assert local autonomy, and the creation of county boroughs has made matters worse. With 62 county councils and 83 county boroughs, the second tier in the administrative hierarchy in England and Wales now comprises 145 units. (For administrative convenience the National Coal Board established nine divisions.) It is desirable that regional authorities should be established and should control planning. If, however, they controlled only planning, they could

* Quoted by J. B. Cullingworth in *Housing in Greater London*, L.S.E., 1961.

do nothing to reform housing administration, nothing to ensure that ten years' residence was not made a qualification for a council house, little to concentrate resources on the areas in the greatest need, and little to improve the standard of architecture.

If the proposed Greater London Council (Greater London would comprise the L.C.C. area, Middlesex, and parts of Hertfordshire, Essex, Kent, and Surrey) were to have the present (concurrent) powers of the L.C.C., then it would truly represent progress. In fact, the L.C.C.'s powers are to be divided, some going up to the Greater London Council, some down to the 33 new enlarged boroughs. It will have to be seen how the Greater London Council uses its planning and housing powers; but if the L.C.C.'s architect's department is to be broken up, and many of the houses and schools it would have designed are to be designed instead in the boroughs, then on that ground alone we are probably better off as we are.

Most people who have studied housing and planning problems would like to see both a drastic revision of the present local-authority boundaries and the introduction of elected regional authorities. Failing such a comprehensive reform, the introduction of unelected regional authorities should both accomplish more and arouse less opposition than the revision of local boundaries. Their powers would be delegated from the central Government and could at no time exceed the powers the central Government had acquired for itself. As with the central Government at present, much of their effective power would derive not from statutory right but from the services and finance they had to offer.

The original autonomy of the local authorities has long since been lost. They do not do things each in their own way. They depend on funds from the Government and do things in the Government's way. When the Government offers a subsidy for ordinary houses, they build ordinary houses. When the Government withdraws the subsidy for ordinary houses and offers subsidies for slum clearance and flats for old people, then they clear slums and build flats for old people. The Government discriminates between them by giving differential and discretionary subsidies, but because there are too many of them for it to assess their needs, it discriminates insufficiently. We have left the local authorities too much autonomy in finance – that is, have left the poorer ones too dependent on their own resources. At the same time we have allowed them too little autonomy in determining their own priorities.

A regional authority could stand to the local authorities much as many successful private companies stand to their subsidiaries. It would control planning and (by virtue of holding the purse-strings) expensive capital development, such as slum clearance and the redevelopment of city centres. If urban renewal is to be undertaken thoroughly and effectively, it cannot be undertaken everywhere at once – any more than the local authorities are able to clear all their slums at once. Clearly the regional authority would devote its capital resources to what it regarded as the most deserving projects (as the L.C.C. has done). For the rest, it would do research and development, offer specialist services, watch comparative costs (it would certainly investigate the wide range in the cost of construction of council houses under different authorities), and pick up good ideas developed by individual authorities and spread them among the others. A local authority wanting its housing or planning administration revised could call in the regional authority's specialists for advice (or, if it were simply a problem of conflicting interests, for arbitration). The regional authority's architect's department, undertaking research and development, would make new ideas, materials, and (it is to be hoped) standardized components available to the local authorities. It would design the buildings in any scheme financed by the regional authority, and it should be ready, for a fee, to design buildings for the local authorities at their request and in accordance with their instructions. (J. M. Richards, joint editor of the *Architectural Review*, has suggested there should be such a relation between the architects' department of the Greater London Council and the new boroughs.*) The regional authority's services would be available to private enterprise – including housing associations.

The power relations between a regional authority and the local authorities would vary greatly according to context. To exercise its planning function, the regional authority would have to be given statutory control at least in matters affecting regional planning as such. Over much large-scale development it would exercise financial control. When offering advice on organization and methods and the like, it would stand to a local authority as consultant to client, except that it would not necessarily draw a fee. In designing buildings at the request of a local authority, it would be that authority's paid architect. With such an idiosyncratic status, regional authorities may even commend themselves to defenders of the British Constitution.

* *Listener*, 11 January 1962.

7 Special Problems

THE HOMELESS

In 1961 Jeremy Sandford was visiting an ex-neighbour at Newington Lodge, Southwark, which afforded temporary accommodation for many of London's homeless. He went away from one of his visits to write the most famous newspaper article of recent years:

Up to three families are crammed into one room at Newington Lodge, and the rooms contain up to thirteen beds. Edna shares two toilets with sixty-four other people. Husbands must find their own accommodation. Feeding is at long tables in a communal dining-hall; and owing to the number of inmates who contract dysentery, new arrivals must queue up three times for the unpleasant ritual of 'swabbing' up the backside. . . .

The doctor told Edna that there was dysentery 'in the walls', and warned her to keep her children as clean as she could. At first she kept her children locked in her room, in order to keep them healthy. But she was paying the L.C.C. £5 19s. for bed and board, her husband was paying for separate lodgings, National Insurance, storage of their furniture, travel, and clothes; and so, rather than starve, she and the children had to go down to the dining-room. . . .

Last time I saw Edna, a change had come over her. It was during visiting hours, and I was meant to be seeing her husband too; but he didn't turn up. 'I had a bit of a row with him. He says he can't bear to set foot in this place, and he can't afford the fares for travel. I said: "What about me? I have to live

here." "There seem to be two kids missing." I said: "Yes,
the ambulance took them. They got the sickness.'" *

By October 1961 the L.C.C. had nearly 3,000 homeless
people, many of them children, living in temporary accommodation. This was two and a half times as many as four
years previously. Besides being formidable in scale, the
problem was new in kind. The homeless were not problem
families. The heads of the families were not even unemployed. They were for the most part unskilled workers with
secure jobs, earning perhaps £12 a week, who had been
evicted from or priced out of their previous homes. Such
other accommodation as was not too expensive they had
been refused, because they had children. The removal of a
large number of rented houses from rent control had contri-
buted to but not caused the problem. The essential cause
was – and remains – a lack of planning. The number of jobs
in London had been allowed to increase, at the same time as
rent control was relaxed and the building of council houses
for general needs was reduced. The resources devoted to
building office-blocks – which create new jobs and hence
draw more people into London – should have been devoted
to building houses. Then, not only would there have been
enough accommodation, but, with demand and supply in
balance, its price would not have been beyond the means of
the able-bodied employed.

The L.C.C. had done everything within the powers allotted to it to remove its surplus population to New Towns and
other areas. The problem of the homeless was not of its
making. Presented with it, it resorted to desperate measures. The conditions at Newington Lodge were not the
result of administrative neglect. Essentially they were deliberate. If the inmates were to have an incentive to move on
and make room for others, they had to be given conditions

* 'Families without a Home', *Observer*, 17 September 1961.

even viler than those they were likely to get in rented accommodation that they could afford. In its application of this policy the L.C.C. laid itself open to criticism. It would surely have been enough *either* to separate husbands from wives, *or* to give the children dysentery. Moreover, the L.C.C. was reduced to moving people out of Newington Lodge after a given time, regardless of whether they had found alternative accommodation. If it was going to return them to the street after a few weeks anyway, it could have let them live decently meanwhile. Since the outcry that followed Jeremy Sandford's article, the L.C.C. has somehow managed to provide far better accommodation for the homeless.

On the charge of complacency, the L.C.C. is entitled to be acquitted. It was its lack of complacency that made it take desperate measures. It knew, as its critics did not, that there were people living in just as bad conditions in its slums and in overcrowded privately-rented accommodation (and that among them were people of chronic ill health, with an even greater need to be re-housed than the inmates of Newington Lodge). It feared, moreover, that however many houses it compulsorily purchased to house the existing homeless, more would appear to take their place, as long as the number of jobs in London was allowed to increase.

Both the responsibility and the complacency were the Government's. So long as the L.C.C. was getting the blame, it seemed not to be concerned about the problem at all. There were even implications that by charging economic rents for council houses the L.C.C. could have driven its more affluent tenants into finding accommodation for themselves, and so have freed enough council houses to accommodate the homeless. People were only living in Newington Lodge because the alternative was to pay anything up to £7 a week for a couple of rooms. To drive out any number of its tenants the L.C.C. would have needed to charge about £10 a week rent for its houses. Is this what the Government intended?

THE OVERCROWDED

We have already considered the slums and the substandard housing. Certain houses popularly regarded as the worst slums are included in neither category. These are the un-converted houses that have been crammed full of tenants to the very great advantage of the landlords – the houses where people sleep several to a room and where several families must share perhaps a single kitchen and a single lavatory. They appear in Ministry publications as 'houses in multiple occupation'. They are properly distinguished from slums, in the official sense, because it is not the houses as such which constitute slums. It is the use to which they have been put which makes them, in the popular sense, slummy. They do not need to be pulled down. They just need to be emp-tied of most of their tenants, cleaned, and painted – and probably, because most of them are large, converted into flats. Overcrowding to this extent occurs in the cities and towns where the housing shortage is acute, and where ac-cordingly nearly all privately-rented property not subject to control is expensive.

The Government seems more concerned about over-crowding than about homelessness. In addition to restoring subsidies for council houses built to relieve overcrowding, it has recently given local authorities wider powers than they had previously to control 'multi-occupied' houses. Local authorities are expected to limit numbers of tenants, and to make landlords install and maintain adequate cook-ing, water, and sanitary facilities. Landlords offending against the new regulations can be fined £20 or sentenced to three months' imprisonment, for a first offence.

Regulations governing multi-occupation are difficult to

enforce, and if they are enforced render people homeless. Indeed the problems of homelessness and overcrowding are different species of the same genus. Only London and Birmingham have had much experience of the problem of homelessness, but it could be created in any number of cities by the rigorous application of anti-overcrowding regulations. Glasgow has families of twelve living in single rooms. It is because of the fear of homelessness that local authorities cannot yet get much cooperation from overcrowded tenants in bringing landlords to book. The problem of multi-occupation will be overcome only when the acute local housing shortages are overcome – whether by building tall blocks of flats, or by moving offices and factories and the people who work in them to places where there is still room for houses – and when the cost of privately-owned uncontrolled housing in the congested areas has been brought within the reach of the unskilled worker.

It is widely supposed that coloured immigrants have been responsible for the degeneration of the multi-occupied houses. Indeed the belief that, when a West Indian is not taking an Englishman's job or council house, he is creating a slum was probably responsible for much of the support for the Immigration Bill. An inquiry in Nottingham, which gained notoriety for its racial troubles, showed that neither disrepair nor overcrowding was more common in immigrants' own houses than in natives', but that a higher proportion of immigrants were living in the multi-occupied houses. What this tells one is that immigrants tend to get the worst of the housing available, in the same way that they tend to get the worst of the jobs available. They do not in fact create unemployment. *The Economist* has shown that (until one introduces an Immigration Bill threatening to keep them out) immigrants come only when there are jobs for them to do – that 'when the jobs are even marginally reduced (as happened in 1958) then the flow is reduced

more than proportionately'.* (When unemployment de-
velops, they may well be the first to be laid off; but this is
only to say that they preserve jobs for Englishmen.) Provided there are jobs for them, their production will cover
the cost of providing houses for them. It is possible that,
being frightened of declaring themselves homeless to official-
dom, they are readier than natives to tolerate (as distinct
from seek or create) the worst excesses of multi-occupation.
If this is so, it merely affords another example of the inter-
changeability of homelessness and overcrowding.

THE OLD

Most old people will say they want a ground-floor flat.
But this simply means they do not like climbing stairs. A
multi-storey block of flats with access balconies and lifts at
Wythenshawe, Manchester, has shown that old people can
feel more secure high above the street, and can prefer to be
away from the noise, particularly when they are within
sight and easy reach of a shopping centre. In short, as soon
as we begin to consider housing for the old, we come up
against the want of market research and, worse still, against
the want of facilities for market research. As any market
researcher knows, it is no good asking people what they
want. Most old people say they want a coal fire, thinking of
gas and electric fires as the alternatives. Tempt them with
central heating and they will hesitate – between their desires
for the familiar and for warmth. Persuade them to accept
central heating, and (provided it is not very expensive to
run) the vast majority of them will never look back. Market
research requires experiment, observation of how people
react to and use things. We have barely begun to build
special housing for the old, and so have had little chance to
observe it in action.

* 25 November 1961.

Do old people want to live among other old people, or in a balanced community containing middle-aged and young adults and children? The housing manager and welfare officer to Chatham Borough Council, Mr R. W. Morris, reported that of 113 old people who were living in council property, 75 declared in interviews that the generations did not mix (mainly because the young want to make more noise), and 38 preferred living near people with children because it 'stopped them getting too crotchety'. But this need not perplex us. Old people are entitled to vary in their preferences. We can feel assured of the widespread demand for housing adapted to old people's needs, and much at least of this demand is for housing schemes devoted to old people, which happens to be the most economical way to build it, and the only practicable way of making the services of a trained warden constantly available. The faster we get on with building it the better.

Probably the best example of housing for old people is provided by the flatlets at Stevenage (to which we referred earlier because they have been built from prefabricated parts). The designs were prepared for Stevenage New Town Development Corporation by the Ministry's development group, after a study by a Ministry sociologist of the experience of tenants, wardens, and housing managers of six existing local-authority flatlet schemes.

Old people want privacy – they want their own homes. They also, most of them, like company to be readily available. The Stevenage scheme conforms to the pattern of old people's housing in comprising flats and common rooms. It also has long corridors in which there are sitting spaces with tables and chairs. There are flats for both couples and single people; those for couples have a living-room and bedroom, those for single people just a bed-sitting-room. Every flat has a kitchen and a lavatory with a wash-basin, but none has its own bath. Baths are shared, there being one to every six flats. This is not only a reasonable economy. It makes possible provision for a variety of disabilities to which old people are prone. It also relieves the occupiers of the flats of the duty of keeping a bath clean. Ground-floor flats have electric underfloor heating, supplemented by a radiant fire; first-floor flats have electric skirting heating. Hot water comes from electrically heated tanks shared between two flats. Much thought has been given in the design of the flats to giving people good lighting and a varied outlook. The common-room – at the centre of the building, adjoining the warden's two-bedroomed house – has been divided into two, to accommodate both television and talk or games, but can be undivided again for parties. The smaller of the divided rooms can be used as a guest-room. There is the usual bell system to the warden's house. Communal refrigerators provide a space for each tenant, and the milkman leaves the milk in them; but mail is delivered to each flat. There are two communal utility rooms fitted with a washing machine, spin-dryer, sink, and heated drying cabinet, with outdoor drying space near by. The site of the scheme adjoins a neighbourhood centre and family housing. The shops and the bus are no distance away.

I have described the Stevenage scheme in some detail because it is not, as it ought to be (and is in Scandinavia), commonplace. In 1956 the Government introduced the £10-a-year subsidy on one-bedroomed dwellings. At that time local authorities were completing about 15,000 one-bedroomed dwellings a year. By 1961, when the housing subsidies were consolidated, this figure had almost been doubled, despite a substantial reduction in the total number of dwellings completed. Though the standard of design varied greatly – and not all one-bedroomed dwellings in fact go to old people – it is clear that a sensible policy was effectively implemented. Yet progress of this order scarcely touches the problem. The National Corporation for the

Care of Old People, which has the most reliable information to draw on, has said:

> Generally speaking the number of dwellings provided annually by local authorities for persons of pensionable age is little more than one-third of what will have to be built annually over the next twenty years for persons of pensionable age if the backlog is to be made up and reasonable demands met.*

This implies about 75,000 new dwellings a year.

At present the old tend to be not only inappropriately housed but plain badly housed. Although there are no up-to-date figures of the amenities possessed by old people, we can be sure that they still have far less than their fair share of baths and flush lavatories – even far less than their fair share of running cold water. And their houses are older and more in need of repair than other people's. Since the old tend to be poor, in pre-war society this might have been accepted as being in the nature of things. But a society concerned with social justice should argue from the fact that it is less hardship for the young to fetch their water in a pail, and should ensure that old people have more amenities rather than less. Just because so many of the old are living in substandard housing which ought to be pulled down when they move, 75,000 new dwellings a year would for a time represent a considerable call on building resources. Eventually, however, large numbers of old people would be moving into special housing from the adequate but inappropriate housing that they now 'under-occupy'. By this time, housing for old people would be helping to solve the housing problem of the young.

What has private enterprise done about housing for the old? To find examples one must go to those towns on the south coast where the middle classes have to some extent

* 13th Annual Report, March 1961, quoted by John Greve in *The Housing Problem*.

solved the problems of retirement by the simple act of con-
gregating: 29·8 per cent of Worthing's population are of
pensionable age (men sixty-five and over, women sixty and
over), which is exactly double the proportion in the population of England and Wales. Worthing has a warm climate, a
flat shopping centre, and 4¾ miles of promenade. In the
early days of its expansion, the retired were no doubt drawn
to it by these considerations alone. Now they are also drawn
by the prospect of living near old colleagues and friends and
enjoying the amenities such as clubs and bowling greens
that have come into being to satisfy the needs of the existing
retired population.

When one compares the housing for the middle-class old
with Stevenage, it is apparent that little if any thought has
been given to their special needs. The housing in Worthing
is of a certain size, and there are large numbers of bungalows with no stairs to walk up, but that is about as far as it
goes. It is true that the retired middle classes find the
problems of old age mitigated. Many can afford cars and
some domestic help. But the problems catch up with them
in the end. In their seventies or eighties they are likely to
find that they need a bit of help or nursing from time to
time, yet are not prepared for the sacrifice of privacy involved in moving into a private home or (even if they can
afford it) a hotel. What they need – and often know they
need, but look for it in vain – are small service flats adapted
to old people's needs. They want their own homes still, but
they want domestic help and straightforward nursing available; they want a restaurant where the cook is willing to
respect idiosyncratic diets; they want a lounge where they
can have coffee or a drink and meet people, without the
effort of going out and the risk of catching cold. There seems
no reason why such accommodation should not be provided
by private enterprise, immediately in towns that attract
numbers of retired people, and ultimately throughout the

country. Private enterprise could be helped to overcome its inertia by the appropriate use of planning regulations. Provision of special housing for the middle-class old would help significantly to solve the general housing problem. For the most part, those who moved into it would be leaving vacant much larger dwellings in good condition.

Since the 1961 Housing Act, more philanthropic housing associations have come into existence to provide housing for the old. There are also signs of development of housing co-operatives among the middle-class retired, for whom they have indeed a double advantage. They are a means both of getting suitable houses built and of getting mortgages for their purchase. Housing associations never die.

The main thing the retired middle classes have that the retired working classes lack is of course the opportunity of moving to Worthing – to a pleasant climate and a plenitude of suitable amenities. If a retired couple want a council flat, they must put their names on a waiting list and stay put. Yet it would be cheaper to put up housing for old people if it were concentrated in certain parts of the country; and by attracting more old people away from the industrial and commercial centres we should ease the housing problem for everyone else. This is yet another reason why responsibility for council housing should be placed more than one tier above the parish council.

THE DISABLED

The legislation at the base of the Welfare State assumed that its old citizens would be either sick or well. In the fifties Jean Graham Hall referred to ‘ “a tragic no-man’s-land ” for old people, in which the half-sick, half-well, find it difficult to obtain adequate provision’.* The very infirm

* *Social Welfare and the Citizen*, edited by Peter Archer, Penguin Books, 1957.

struggled ineffectually to look after themselves in their own homes; or lived in welfare homes where the privacy of single rooms, which had been provided with the best intentions, amounted to a sentence of solitary confinement; or were kept in badly needed hospital beds, for want of anywhere else to send them.

Once the problem was recognized, something was done about it. To enable the infirm to live more happily in their own homes, the National Old People's Welfare Council gave increasing attention to the provision of visitors, night sitters, nurses, home helps, 'meals on wheels' services, and visiting chiropodists and physiotherapists. A number of welfare homes were adapted to the needs of the infirm by reducing the 'privacy' and increasing the medical and nursing attention. Experiments were made whereby infirm old people needing a great deal of attention lived alternately a few weeks with their families and a few weeks in welfare homes, their families thus being assured of a periodical rest from responsibilities that might otherwise have proved too exacting.

All this is to the good. But the problem of the infirm old and of the disabled of all ages is one that needs to be met at an architectural level. A start has at least been made. In 1961 a conference on 'Architectural Design for the Disabled' was organized by the Building Exhibition and the National Fund for Research into Poliomyelitis and other Crippling Diseases. This both disseminated knowledge about the subject and stimulated interest in it. And the Polio Research Fund, in association with the R.I.B.A., has awarded a research scholarship to an architect, Selwyn Goldsmith, for the study of the design of equipment, fittings, and buildings for the disabled.

It might seem that we are dealing here with a social service that is pure social charity, that must add to public expenditure without bringing any return. This is far from true.

A speaker at the conference on 'Architectural Design for the Disabled' pointed out that good basic design is often a superior substitute for more expensive gadgetry. Summing up, the chairman of the conference, Sir Walter Puckey, argued from experience in industry that design to help the disabled was anything but expensive. To neglect it was to create what another speaker in a wheelchair had described as 'architectural barriers' to a normal and useful life for the disabled, and so prevent them from making their own productive contribution to the community.

What, though, of those whose disablement must prevent them from making a significant productive contribution, even with the architect's and designer's assistance? It is here in fact that the community can make the greatest saving at the same time as doing the greatest good. At present the disabled in this category are supported permanently in hospital. If they could be reunited with their families in special blocks of flats with nursing annexes, their charge on the community would be less. Abraham Marcus, the medical correspondent of the *Observer*, has named victims of polio with respiratory paralysis, and people suffering from multiple sclerosis, as among the young chronic sick who could live in such flats.* They already do so in Denmark. A block of flats was opened in Copenhagen in 1960 as a result of a study of respiratory patients who had survived the Danish polio epidemic of 1952. The nursing annexe has breathing machines that patients can sleep in at night or reach quickly by lift in an emergency. The Danish Government pays generous allowances to the relatives who look after the patients in these flats – a widowed mother looking after her sick child gets £35 a month in addition to her rent. Even so, it apparently costs a third less to keep patients in their own homes than in hospitals.

In practice, too, housing for the disabled must bring a

* *Observer*, 22 October 1961.

direct return to the community in design. Many of the problems it presents to the architect are but everyday problems in a more acute form (and of course in designing for the disabled the architect has to keep in mind the needs of non-disabled relatives). Not the least important aspect of design for the disabled is the reduction of hazards. Non-slip surfaces, safety taps for gas and electric cookers, safe and easy-to-turn handles, windows that open easily – these are just some of the attributes of housing for the disabled to which architects have already given attention and which we can expect ultimately to be incorporated in all housing, with a consequent reduction in the present serious rate of accidents in the home.

8 The Property 'Racket'

THE Alliance Building Society wrote of sites for flats commanding 'fabulous prices' – £23,000 per acre in Reading, £40,000 in Wembley, £48,000 in Worthing. Land in Yorkshire, indistinguishable in quality, may cost barely £1,000 an acre. Figures published by the Cooperative Permanent Building Society* indicate that in the three years 1959–61 the price of new houses in Great Britain as a whole rose by 25 per cent, while house-building costs rose by only 11 per cent – and this comparison makes no allowance for increased productivity in the building industry. In the same period the price of existing houses originally worth £3,000 or less in London and £2,500 or less elsewhere rose by 14–15 per cent. (Being the average for the whole country, this figure takes account of depressed areas, where the prices of houses are falling.) The prices of more expensive houses rose by 31 per cent – by more than the cost of new houses. There are houses in London which even during the acute shortage of the early post-war years sold for only £2,500 and are now selling for over £8,000.

'How far distant is the day', asked the Alliance Building Society, 'when the last piece of land scheduled for housing has been sold? In many areas, it would seem that that day is very close – if it has not already passed. . . .' In explaining a scarcity of land for housing, it is no longer good enough to say that the demand for it is for ever increasing while the

* *House Prices in 1961*, Occasional Bulletin No. 47, February 1962.

supply remains constant. Nowadays we are supposed to have planning. We say where houses may be built and where they shall not be built. If the amount of land scheduled for housing has proved inadequate, we must ask why, and we shall do so when we discuss planning.

For the moment we shall take the scarcity of land and the consequent rise in land values as given. Among those who have benefited from it are the local authorities and the development corporations – the New Towns have shown a loss on the revenue account but a large profit on capital account. Anyone who owned land, whether or not it was built on, at the end of the war, and anyone who has bought property or land since, is likely (though by no means certain) to have gained – to have made money for nothing. While both landlords and owner-occupiers have therefore gained, the people who have gained most are those who buy and sell land frequently – the property-developers and those who speculate in land without developing it (usually selling to developers).* They study the market in land. They can usually judge where the value of land is going to increase fast, and where it can be further increased by development. They know of the planning decisions which affect the values of particular properties. They may offer an owner £1,000 more than he thinks his property is worth and £2,000 less than it is actually worth. It is sometimes forgotten that an owner-occupier whom they have done out of £2,000 was no more entitled to it than they are.

There have of course been certain rackets in the real sense of the word. Because property-developers are dealing in property all the time – because, in fact, property-development

* Seven years ago Mr Eddie Meadows, a property-developer, bought a 32-acre plot of vacant ground at Hounslow. As the result of a recent planning decision its value is estimated at £3 million. This appears to be the record profit. It was not, however, money for nothing, since the chances were that he would lose on the investment.

is their business – the money they make is regarded as income and is taxable, whereas the profit made by an owner-occupier or landlord from an occasional sale of property is regarded as a capital gain and is not. Chancellors of the Exchequer have spent a long time trying to catch up with the various means that property-developers have found of presenting their profits as capital gains. When Mr Selwyn Lloyd announced in the 1962 Budget that profits on land or property turned over within three years would be taxable, he was not so much introducing a new law as seeking to enforce existing laws.

A property-developer's life is not entirely risk-free. He may suffer from planning decisions that he has not expected, or he may simply miscalculate. A landlord or his agent may get planning approval in principle for a development scheme, and quote this approval in selling his land. Later investigation may lead to provision for open spaces and roads restricting the property-developer's scope. Property-developers have on occasion overestimated the demand for housing on a particular site, or have put up housing for which not enough purchasers could get mortgages. But the fact remains that the market in land is an extraordinarily good one, and the property-developers know it better than anyone else. They can even to some extent – and this qualifies as a racket – manipulate the market. In a rapidly rising and hence inevitably imperfect market, a single precedent can determine values. If a property company sells a piece of land by auction, and arranges for someone to bid twice its market value, it will very likely be able to sell adjoining pieces of land to genuine buyers at similar prices. Contrived precedents can also help to determine the prices of new houses.

A rapidly rising and imperfect market also gives scope to an unscrupulous estate agent. An estate agent offers vendors advice on the price they should ask, and there is nothing to stop him buying privately a house he is selling professionally. The recently established National Association of Estate Agents wants the Government to make this practice an offence. At the inaugural meeting of the Association, Roy Brooks said he had just sold a property for £2,500 after another agent had told the vendor he could not get more than £750 for it. Not all this discrepancy can be attributed to copy-writing skill.

While the people who have gained most from rising land values are the property-developers, property-development as such is no more a racket than is buying a house to live in and then selling it for three times as much when one moves. Both are easy ways of making money, which any community is foolish not to tax heavily, and particularly a community that taxes earned income heavily. Before we consider what kind of tax might be imposed, we must examine some other potentialities of taxation.

THE OFFICE PROBLEM

Property-developers put up expensive housing and shops, but they are happiest putting up offices. With the abandonment of building licences in 1954, central London became, in the words of the Town and Country Planning Association, 'the property speculators' Klondike'.* We had been at great pains to move factories out of London, but had given little thought to controlling offices. Now offices appeared on bombed sites, and old offices still standing were pulled down so that new ones could be put up in their stead. New offices appeared wherever planning permission could be obtained for them. The L.C.C. was often inhibited about refusing planning permission because of the compensation it would have to pay for loss of development rights. In addition, it seems to have underestimated the amount of floor space –

* *The Paper Metropolis*, 1962.

and hence the number of employees – that could be accommodated per unit of cubic content.

The result is that ever more people are working in central London and ever fewer living in it. Ever more people are making ever longer journeys to work at ever greater expense. Because of the consequent traffic problem, it has been made difficult for motorists to find anywhere to park their cars, in the hope that they will resort to the already overcrowded trains and buses. Since we know that one of the things people most want of housing is that it should afford them a short and comfortable journey to work, these are developments that we must consider.

The 'London region' is now an area with a radius of fifty miles and a population of $12\frac{1}{2}$ million. Two-thirds of this population live in the London conurbation, which has a radius of twelve to sixteen miles. The population within the County of London at the centre of the conurbation has fallen from 4·4 million in 1931 to 3·2 million today. The fall since 1952 has been more than 150,000. Since 1952 the population of the rest of the conurbation has remained static, while the population in the 20–35-mile belt round the conurbation has risen by 870,000 or 26 per cent (compared with an increase in England and Wales of 5 per cent). On present trends, it could increase from 4·3 million to 6·5 million over the next twenty years. At least 400,000 new houses would be needed, of which less than half could be built on land already allocated to residential use. The conurbation already has 80 per cent of the region's jobs, to only 65 per cent of its population. The number of people travelling into the central area of London between seven and ten in the morning is now 1,294,000, an increase of 116,000 since 1953. These figures mock the post-war policy of dispersal of both population and jobs embodied in 'overspill' and the New Towns.

Office zones and plot ratios in the central area have been

reduced. For the rest the Government has relied on exhortation. It lent its support to a conference called by the Town and Country Planning Association in 1958 on 'Office Location in the London Region', at which the theme was that most firms could decentralize their records, statistics, and research in the direction of the outer suburbs, the New Towns, and the expanding country towns near London, and could manage with a *pied-à-terre* in London for receiving foreign visitors and for leaving for London Airport from. What they lost in prestige by not having a full-scale London office they could regain by introducing closed-circuit television for Board meetings of scattered directors. And just think of the money they could save.

This appeal to enlightened self-interest was not entirely misconceived. Because both salaries and rates are higher in central London, a firm can at present save £140 per employee per year by having its offices in a New Town instead; and there are further gains in better timekeeping and reduced sickness. More than eighty concerns have in fact moved their offices to places between ten and forty miles from the centre, and all declare that the advantages outweigh the disadvantages. Why do not more firms move out? Among those that rent their offices, communications and the desire for prestige are the main reasons. But not all offices are rented. One firm told the Town and Country Planning Association that 'a new building in the middle of London, though much more costly, would probably appreciate in value, whereas one outside might not, and would in any case be less easily disposed of if this were ever necessary'. So long as the present state of affairs is allowed to continue, the capital value of office blocks – as of all buildings in central London – will steadily increase, and can be set against the £140 per employee per year that could be saved by moving out.

What should be done to alter the present state of affairs?

The Town and Country Planning Association proposes 'a mixture of strengthened planning controls and new financial measures'. Its strengthened planning controls include, as well as more restricted zoning of new office development, the abolition of the present right to increase the cubic content of rebuilt offices by 10 per cent. This is almost an assertion that planning, as distinct from control, is impossible. By allowing rebuilt offices their extra 10 per cent cubic content, and restricting the total number of offices in proportion, one could conserve space for houses, roads, shops, restaurants, and so forth. The Town and Country Planning Association rejected a system of Office Development Certificates by analogy with the Industrial Development Certificates that have to be obtained before factories can be built, on the ground that 'this type of employment control would be harder to apply effectively and fairly to offices than to factories'. But it recommends the use of a quota system for controlling the amount of office space created in different areas by new building and rebuilding. Quotas are surely open to the same objections as Office Development Certificates, unless financial measures assure that the demand for new office space is reduced to the level set by the quotas, when the quotas are unnecessary.

Of financial measures, the Town and Country Planning Association says:

An important aim of public policy should be to bring home to employers the indirect costs and inconveniences which are brought about through the over-concentration of employment. In the case of London these indirect costs are very considerable, embracing as they do the enormous costs of road improvements, the specially large subsidies for multi-storey housing, and the capital charges on transport improvements which may increasingly have to be borne by the taxpayer. There are also the high rents and housing hardships caused by over-concentration, and the fatigue of lengthening journeys to work. We believe that part of the bill for the congestion can properly be presented to those who cause it through the introduction of some special tax or levy. This would also drive home to office employers the advantages of decentralization.

The Town and Country Planning Association advocates two very worthwhile financial measures: a levy on new floor space such as is paid in certain zones in Paris; and a payroll tax in the County of London. The payroll tax 'could take the form of an annual payment to the Government by the employer in respect of every employee, excepting, say, the first twenty'. A payroll tax is also advocated by *The Economist*. With revenue coming in from new taxes, of whatever kind, the present obligation to pay substantial compensation for the loss of development rights need not be such a deterrent to the refusal of planning permission for new offices. With a tax of the kind that we are now going to consider, the value of the lost development rights – and hence of the compensation – would be smaller.

A LAND TAX

Unlike a once-for-all levy, a continuing tax on offices in certain areas – whether a payroll tax or a tax based on land value – would have the incidental but important effect of reducing the capital value of offices in those areas. Any increase in the outgoings associated with property must reduce its capital value. A freehold property will sell for more than an equivalent leasehold property on which ground rent must be paid every year (and would do so even if the lease were indefinite). Similarly the rates payable on a property reduce its capital value. In principle the capital value of all properties could be kept constant by large enough increases in rates.

Rates are not in fact suitable for this purpose. They are

still resolutely regarded as a means of raising revenue for local authorities, despite the fact that the local authorities now rely heavily on contributions from central funds for their revenue. Rates were conceived as the simplest way of raising local taxes from the wealthy. They were never an equitable means. Wealth is not proportionate to property. A bookmaker may run a very lucrative business from a small office, while a firm in heavy industry needs vast factories as well as substantial offices in order to make an equivalent income. A rich owner-occupier will pay less rates in proportion to his income than one who could only just afford to buy a house.

Inevitably the basic system of rating and valuation has been interfered with from time to time. Agricultural land is exempt from rates. At present industrial property is rated at 50 per cent of its value, commercial property at 80 per cent of its value, and house property at 100 per cent of its value. Whereas, however, industrial and commercial properties are rated on their values as assessed in 1956, house properties are rated on their 1939 values. In 1963 we are in principle due to get off to a fresh start, with all three kinds of properties being rated at 100 per cent of their current values. It is clear, however, that industrial valuations have been increased disproportionately. On average the householder's share of the rates will be slightly smaller than now, though there will be wide variations according to the distribution of industry and commerce.

Whether or not certain kinds of property are wholly or partly exempted from rates, inequities must exist both between different kinds and within each kind. Rates cannot even be defended as an effective means of encouraging the profitable use of scarce land. Rateable value is not in proportion to the value of the land on which a property stands, but to the value both of the land and of the property itself. If property is improved, its rateable value goes up. This is to say that if a better use is made of the land on which it stands, higher rates must be paid. To this extent the rating system discourages the better use of land. It is even true that rates do not have to be paid on a property if it is standing empty, which is encouragement to sheer waste.

Despite growing criticism of rates as a means of raising revenue, it is probably not yet practical politics to scrap them, least of all in order to substitute a higher tax based solely on land values. Governments are always reluctant to abandon an existing form of taxation, on the rational ground that the electorate object to all taxes and object much more to new ones than to those they are used to. In addition, it would be difficult to persuade the local authorities that the proceeds of the new higher tax did not all belong to them. The local authorities would in fact have grounds for fearing that, once it was conceded that some of the new tax should be paid into central or regional funds, they would have no source of revenue that they could really call their own. It may therefore be necessary, for a time, to leave the rating system intact and to impose a new tax independent of local-authority finance. We cannot adapt Schedule A to our purpose. Like rates, it is based on the value of properties, not merely on the value of land. Unlike rates, it is so based for a good reason: it is an essential part of income tax. The abolition of Schedule A on owner-occupied houses, by reducing the owner-occupier's outgoings, will simply send the prices of houses even higher.

Could a general capital-gains tax on properties be made to work? The exact capital gain to be made on a property is not known till it is sold. Not to impose the tax until properties were sold would, however, discourage everyone from selling. So long as the owner did not sell, he would retain any increase in the capital value of his property. Rather than sell it and be taxed on his capital gain, he would let it at a rent in proportion to its new higher value. If he wanted capital, he would raise a mortgage on its new higher value.

A capital-gains tax would need to be levied whether or not property was sold. It would need to be levied periodically on the basis of an assessment of increased values. Suppose for the moment that we proposed a capital-gains tax of 100 per cent, and that the value of property in a particular area is assessed as having risen by 10 per cent since the last valuation. On the office block that had previously been worth £400,000 the tax would be £40,000. On the house that had previously been worth £4,000 the tax would be £400. Clearly this would be overdoing it. In order to pay a tax of this magnitude, many owner-occupiers and some landlords and companies might be forced to try to realize their capital gains by selling their properties – when, apart from the disruption caused, the slump in the property market would take away much of the capital gain and with it the justification for the tax. The only alternative would be for the property-owners to borrow a large proportion of the money for their taxes from the banks. British banks would probably refuse to lend the money to the owner-occupiers, who would have to admit to the disgrace of being up to their ears in debt in the first place. One could not expect all property-owners to get additional mortgages for marginal amounts every time there was a revaluation.

A capital-gains tax of 100 per cent is just not practicable. Nor is one of 75 per cent, or one of 50 per cent. The greatest that could be imposed is probably one of 10 per cent. Given a 10 per cent increase in values, this would mean a tax of 1 per cent on the original values – of £40 on the £4,000 house and of £4,000 on the £400,000 office block. It would mean that the owner-occupier was getting away with £360 of capital gain and the company owning the office block with £36,000.

We need not despair. Our single capital-gains levy can be

converted into a continuing tax equivalent to the interest on
it. In effect the State can provide indefinite mortgages on
the capital gains that it claims. Instead of charging 100 per
cent once, we can charge say 5 per cent a year for ever – or
until the next assessment shows a further increase in capital
value, when we increase the tax in proportion, or a decrease
in capital value, when we decrease it in proportion. In
short, our capital-gains tax ceases to look like a capital-
gains tax at all, and looks more like the rates.

It is not in fact a capital-gains tax. Not only does it ignore
the prices at which properties change hands. The assess-
ments on which it is based ignore differences in the values of
neighbouring properties of identical size and purpose (and
here the tax differs also from the rates). They take account
only of the general value of property in each district – that
is to say, of the value of land in each district. The tax is
imposed (and here again it differs from the rates) not on all
land values but only on increases in land value after the
introduction of the tax. It varies with the size and purpose
of properties but not with their state of repair or of empti-
ness. Indeed it need not always depend on whether a
property exists. If planning permission had been granted for
an office block of a certain size to be built on a site (and a
reasonable time allowed for building), the tax would be
imposed as though it had been built. (A developer could
always give up his planning permission.) To summarize,
the tax would depend only on the demand for land, on the
use of land made before planning powers were assumed,
and on planning permission. We may as well call it a land
tax.

What would the actual figures be? With a tax of 5 per
cent a year on a hypothetical capital gain of 10 per cent, the
owner of the £400,000 office block would pay £2,000 a year
and the owner of the £4,000 house would pay £20 a year.
The effect of such a tax would be that there were no capital

gains at all. The £400,000 office block would remain worth
£400,000, because the buyer who was prepared to pay
£440,000 must now invest £40,000 (at 5 per cent) in order
to produce his £2,000 a year tax. Similarly, the £4,000
house would remain worth £4,000. We shall certainly avoid
the term 'capital-gains tax'. It would seem like adding
insult to injury.

If one argues from the premise that private property in
land is as inviolate as private property in toothbrushes,
then it follows as the night the day that a land tax is unjust.
But there are few who do argue from this premise today.
For everyone else it is the lack of a land tax which is unjust.
Those paying a land tax must regard it as the cost of
continuing to consume something – land in a certain
area – which is becoming more expensive because more
scarce.

Revaluation of properties for the application of a land
tax would have to be carried out more frequently than for
rating purposes, at least in areas where the value of land was
increasing rapidly and in areas where it was falling.
Revaluation would not, however, be very difficult or expensive. It would not involve assessing every property. We
should be concerned only with the value of the land on
which properties stood, not with the values of the properties
themselves. For the most part revaluation could be conducted by sampling – by assessing the value of a proportion
of unimproved properties. These values would of course
reflect any increase in the value of the land on which they
stood attributable to the improvement of neighbouring properties. Particular properties would need to be assessed only
where there had been some great redevelopment scheme, or
where planning permission for a change of the use of land
had been granted. A constant check on the accuracy of the
assessors would be provided by the prices at which unimproved properties changed hands. On the basis of taxing the

full increase in capital value, these prices should remain constant.

In practice it would be wise to allow for short-term fluctuations in value and for a margin of error by the assessors – and to make some concession to landowners' feelings on the matter – by taxing less than the full increase. I would propose a tax on from 60 to 80 per cent of the increase, according to the speed of increase. Suppose, to keep the figures simple, that one taxed 75 per cent of the increase. The tax on the £400,000 office block would then be £1,500 and the price for which it would be sold (provided the valuation was correct) would be £410,000. Similarly the tax on the £4,000 house would be £15 a year, and it could be sold for £4,100. A small profit for the owner-occupier – for the company owning and occupying its office block as well as for the householder – is perhaps desirable as a contribution to the costs of moving. One of the ways in which the tax must fulfil its purposes is by driving companies and householders out of districts where they cannot really afford to be, and there is sense in letting them have enough money to pay their moving expenses.

There will still then be capital gains to be made, and substantial ones at that. The £10,000 profit on the office block and the £100 profit on the house could be made in many places in a couple of years. Over and above this, there will be capital gains to be made from increases in the value of particular properties. Such increases may be attributable to structural improvements, or to growing public appreciation of design. Capital gains of this kind are not money for nothing. None the less they are money, and there is no rational argument why they should be less subject to tax than wages and salaries. In so far as they are made by people or companies – that is, property-developers – whose whole-time job it is to make them, they are already taxed (or are meant to be). In so far as they are not already taxed, they should either be treated as income (with provision to spread them over several years) or be made subject to a general capital-gains tax.

A DIFFERENTIAL TAX

The imposition of a land tax would of itself do a great deal to disperse the demand for property – to reduce the demand in the centres of the big cities and to increase the demand in the suburbs and the country surrounding them and also in the lesser cities and the towns. To the economies already available to firms that move all or part of their offices out of the centres of the big cities would be added the avoidance of a heavy land tax; and they would have lost one of their incentives for staying put – the fact that the capital value of their offices was increasing so rapidly.

If the demand for offices in London or any other big city remained excessive, no very great problem would be presented. There would be nothing sacrosanct about the range of 60 to 80 per cent of increased value (or any other chosen figures) on which a land tax would be based. Once having brought a land tax into existence, it would be an easy matter to apply it differentially, whether between one area and another, or one form of building and another, such as offices and houses. Most differential taxes lead, via attempts at tax avoidance, to administrative complications. Property definitions are singularly clear-cut. Just as land is clearly distinguishable from other forms of capital, so is land in one area clearly distinguishable from land in another, and it is difficult to disguise offices as houses.

We can be confident of bringing London's office problem under control with a sufficiently rigorous application of a land tax. If we based the tax on offices on 100 per cent (or more) of the increase in capital value, we should see a considerable improvement. And other forms of property besides offices can be differentiated against. In areas where the building of offices and factories was desired, the tax could be increased on houses and shops.

These proposals ought to be equally appealing to the Left and to the Right. The Left is concerned to stop people making money for nothing, and to have sufficient planning to ensure that people can get homes reasonably near to their work. The Right is concerned to preserve the price mechanism, and to minimize bureaucratic interference; and it is in this spirit that *The Economist* has advocated a special tax on offices in central London. The Right is justly fearful of the Left's propensity to think in terms of physical controls – to want to limit office building by a system of licensing requiring a firm to demonstrate to a bureaucrat why it needs to be in London. The Right-wing argument is that people themselves know better than bureaucrats whether they need to live or have an office in a certain place. But the Right usually lacks the courage of its convictions when the preservation of the price mechanism requires the increase of taxes. *Change and Challenge*, the report of a Conservative committee on town and country planning, implies that control of the location of offices would be the lesser evil.

In fact taxes are superior in every respect. Whereas the application of controls is administratively costly, taxes raise revenue. Given that the use of land is determined by planning, taxes do, as *The Economist* contends, leave the decisions to the people best able to make them. The only decision that need be made by a bureaucrat is the extent to which office-building is to be discouraged (and if one has a high non-differential land tax in operation in the first place, the differential tax against offices can be relatively less severe). Thereafter the decisions will be made by managing directors. The firms that remain in or come to London will be those that by the prevailing business criteria can justify the expense. At present they include many that bought their offices long ago and have not noticed that by selling them and investing the proceeds in gilt-edged they could get a return higher than their current business profits.

If we wanted, we could apply our land tax not only differentially but negatively. In those areas (they are few) where the value of land is falling, we could make proportionate yearly payments to property-owners. This could be regarded partly as a matter of justice – the corollary of depriving the more fortunate property-owners of the increased value of land – and partly as a matter of planning policy. It would encourage people to remain in or to move to the depressed areas. In particular it would reduce the accelerating effect whereby people sell properties not because they want to but because they realize values are falling and want to restrict their losses.

Equipped with our flexible land tax, we are now ready to discuss planning, but first we must consider how the problem of land values has been tackled in the past, and how else it might yet be tackled in the future.

OR NATIONALIZATION?

What was regarded as the most important planning measure passed by the Labour Government was contained in the financial provisions of the 1947 Act: all development rights in land were nationalized. To be pedantic, means of vesting increases in the value of land in the State are not planning. They can be introduced on their merits, unaccompanied by planning. One cannot, however, introduce effective planning without first solving the problem of land values. The Labour Government recognized this in principle, but failed to solve the problem in practice. It took account only of development value, not of increases in the value of land already developed. It provided for compensation to be paid to the owners of land which had a significant development value in 1947. Future increases in the value of land attributable to development were to be collected in the form of a 100 per cent 'development charge' on the grant of planning permission. The market in land thereafter collapsed.

As building was freed from controls, the market in land might well have revived, even with the 100 per cent development charge, and it would almost certainly have revived if the development charge had been reduced to 75 per cent. But in the 1953 Town and Country Planning Act the Conservative Government abolished the development charge altogether, creating the situation we have today – a land boom that has actually been aggravated by planning measures. Subsequent Town and Country Planning Acts have provided that compensation should be paid to landowners for loss suffered from planning restrictions, and that owners of land acquired compulsorily should be compensated at the full market value. It is the working of these Acts – particularly when landowners have been granted compensation in respect of potential development for which they might have received planning permission – which has caused most indignation on the Left. Given the abolition of the development charges, the subsequent Acts are completely defensible. It is one thing to want to deprive all landowners of their unearned capital gains. It is another to give local authorities the power to do down individual landowners by compulsory purchase. If the 75 per cent land tax we have discussed were in operation, prices paid under compulsory purchase would have to take account both of the untaxed 25 per cent of the increase in capital value and of 25 per cent of the potential increase as a result of planning permission for development that might have been granted to the owner. This is not the least reason why a land tax should be high.

The Labour Party produced its second unsatisfactory scheme for solving the problem of land values in *Signposts* *for the Sixties*, published in 1961. Since it tacitly abandoned the scheme within a fortnight of its publication, we need not discuss it. The alternative to a straightforward land tax is now the scheme proposed by a group of experts in *Socialist Commentary*.*

Under this, the freehold of all land would be nationalized, freehold land being converted into leasehold with the State as ground landlord. Initially no ground rent would be paid. Valuers would assess the values of all properties and would also give a 'statutory life' to each building from nil to eighty years according to its condition. This statutory life of a building would determine the length of an initial lease. Statutory leases would incorporate rent-revision clauses enabling the State to fix rents, at intervals of seven years, recovering a proportion (50 per cent is suggested) of the increase in the land values for the community. On the expiry of the initial statutory leases, but not before, compensation would be paid for the loss of the freehold. Compensation would be based on the value of the site for its existing use at the vesting date plus a proportion (again 50 per cent is suggested) of the subsequent increase in its value. If planning permission for a change of use of a building or for redevelopment of the land were granted, a new lease would have to be negotiated, and the State would have discretion in fixing the terms of such leases. In general, where permission was granted for new development (of agricultural land), rents would be fixed to recover 80 per cent of the increased value for the community.

In the absence of an alternative, I should myself vote for this scheme with a good heart. Whether one thinks in terms of taxation or of nationalization, the problems to be overcome lead one to much the same conclusions. A land tax could be regarded as ground rent, and the ground rent payable to the State as lessor could be regarded as a tax. Either

* September 1961.

would require the periodical revaluation of properties. Nonetheless the differences between the two schemes are real, and I believe the advantages are with a tax.

With a tax, the State does not acquire the obligation to buy the freehold of all land. The State would gain from holding all freehold only if a time were to come after which all further increase in land values were retained for the community. This is not proposed; nor would it be practicable. The new leases issued on expiry of the initial ones would again have seven-year rent-revision clauses, and the revised rents would again recover only a proportion of increased land values. Why, in any case, should compensation for the freehold, paid on the expiry of an initial lease, include 50 per cent of the increase in the value of the land since the vesting date? Only 50 per cent of the increase in value is to be absorbed in ground rents, and 25 per cent (50 per cent of the residual 50 per cent) is to be paid out in compensation. Of the increase in value between the vesting date and the expiry of a lease (which can be anything up to eighty years) the owner of the land will keep 75 per cent. When allowance is made for the fact that ground rents are to be adjusted only once every seven years, he will in fact keep more than 75 per cent. Compensation should surely be based solely on the value at the vesting date. If it cannot be paid at the time in the form of Government bonds, then it should be paid on the expiry of an initial lease, plus compound interest at the gilt-edged rates prevailing during the intervening period.

The biggest weakness of the scheme is the statutory life accorded to each building. Determining the useful life of each building would be a far more difficult task for assessors than merely determining its current value. It would be so difficult that it could hardly be performed fairly. It is scarcely worth making the point that valuing properties as distinct from land would discourage improvements. Towards the end of the statutory life decreed for his property, the owner would not even have an incentive to preserve it in good condition.

The greatest advantage of a tax is its flexibility. One can increase it whenever and wherever one wants, on all properties or only on certain kinds. It is true that the *Socialist Commentary* scheme provides for the re-negotiation of leases on a change of use of a building or the redevelopment of land, and hence for differential rents. This would make possible a differential charge on a new office block, but not on an existing one, which would be inequitable as well as less effective (and less revenue-raising) than a tax.

The worst of the proposals in *Socialist Commentary* – they are not, fortunately, an essential part of the scheme – are those concerning owner-occupied houses. If an owner-occupier's lease is not renewed (because the land on which it stands is wanted for redevelopment) he is to be given compensation based on the freehold value of the land and buildings as at the time of the expiry of the lease, subject only to an allowance for any ground rent then payable. Add to this the careful statement that 'It would be a matter of policy to decide whether owner-occupiers should be subject to a rent-revision clause', and the fact that no one would pay rent initially, and existing owner-occupiers look like being left as well off as they are now. Of the three different kinds of householders, owner-occupiers are the richest, are the only kind whose expenditure on housing is acquiring them capital value, and they receive, in income-tax reliefs, very considerable financial assistance from the State; and sixteen clever socialists take time off from nationalizing the land to protect owner-occupiers' interests.

9 Planning

DURING the early post-war years, the political connotations of planning made many architects defend Stalin and many Conservatives defend overcrowding. Unfortunately there has been no equivalent of the Twentieth Party Congress to help Conservatives clarify their thoughts. The present Government has come as near to abandoning planning as is possible in a small, densely populated, industrial country.

Town (and country) planning is as desirable – indeed as necessary – in a *laissez-faire* economy as in a socialist economy. It is possible and reasonable to believe in town planning without believing in the planning of the economy as a whole. Everyone believes that the law should prevent his neighbour from erecting a skyscraper that would put his own house in semi-darkness, and town planning is only an extension of this principle. We must not let individual towns develop unplanned, for the same reason as we would not let several architects design different rooms in a single house. And, just as coordination is necessary in building neighbouring houses in order to preserve light and open space and good appearance, and prevent the multiplication of pipes, so the relations between different towns and between town and country need to be controlled, so that not only space but jobs and schools and hospitals, shops and roads and railways, are all kept in proportion.

The powers assumed by planners over the individual are only negative. He may be told he cannot build a house where he wants, even that he must give up a house he has

F

been living in (for example, so that it may be pulled down to make room for a road). But he is not told where he must live. Because of planning he can in fact rely on having a greater variety of environments to choose from. Planning need not even involve many negative instructions to the individual. By definition, planning means only assessing future needs and deciding how they are to be satisfied. The implication is that action will be taken to ensure satisfaction and fulfilment, but, as we saw in the last chapter, the action may just as well take the form of financial measures as of arbitrary bureaucratic decisions. At its best, planning means so contriving things that the choices made by individuals will be compatible with the interests of the community. 'Controls', such as building licences, are no part of planning at all. They are measures employed by all governments whatever their political persuasions, in times of emergency. Planning helps to avoid emergencies, and hence helps to avoid resort to controls.

Since the 1947 Town and Country Planning Act, all land has been subject to planning control. Since planning is such a splendid thing, and since we have not lacked planning powers, we have to explain what has gone wrong. Why has land for housing been scarce in many areas? We have already noted that the planning processes have been undermined by the failure to control land values and the need to pay substantial compensation for loss of development rights where planning permission is refused. It is also true that the planning processes themselves have gone wrong.

The 1947 Act required all local authorities to produce development plans for their areas. Once development plans had been approved by the Minister, planning permissions granted by the local authorities had to conform to them. The Act provided for review of the plans every five years, and also for their amendment at any time in between. In the event, the number of new households has increased faster than was expected at the end of the war. This was one reason why more houses were needed than were built. For the same reason, more land was needed to erect them on than had been allowed for. In some areas the land allocated for housing for twenty years was used up in ten. Quick revision of the plans was therefore necessary.

The discovery that the plans had been based on seriously false estimates more or less coincided with the Government's great reappraisal and its decision to reduce house-building. Local authorities were discouraged from allocating more land for housing and were exhorted to introduce or extend 'green belts'. This is a form of 'control' with a good deal less to commend it than building licences. As a short-term expedient to gain time, while measures were introduced to restrict the demand for land for housing in certain areas, it would have made sense. Since no such measures were introduced or even contemplated, it inevitably increased the scarcity of land. Belatedly, the Minister issued a circular in 1961 requiring all local authorities to review their development plans immediately, and pointing out that green belts must be balanced by provision for development elsewhere.

In some areas scarcity has been aggravated by a considerable discrepancy between land allocated for housing and land available for housing. Not all the owners of land allocated for housing may wish to sell it. But this again need not have mattered if the plans had been revised in accordance with the known facts. Either land could have been acquired by compulsory purchase, or the allocation of land for housing could have been increased.

To advocate planning is not to be obliged to defend bad planning. But in fact nothing that has happened since the war has detracted from the case for planning. Without planning, London would have had even more offices and the London region more industry. The development plans, for all their imperfections and misuse, have kept a great deal of land for housing and done something to ensure the provision of amenities. They have prevented much extension of the pre-war 'sprawl' along the main roads and railways, and the spaces made by bombs could have been filled in with even less regard to aesthetic considerations than they have been. (In America, in the absence of planning, speculative housing estates have been pulled down after less than ten years, to make room for roads.) It is true that far too many local planning decisions have been made by people who believe that pseudo-Tudor is splendid, that the speculative semi-detached is what is to be expected, and that anything else is cranky and unseemly. So far, planning powers have probably been used to stop more really good houses from being built than really bad ones. Even so, the essential criticism to be made of post-war planning is that it has prevented harm rather than done good.

The kind of comprehensive development envisaged by the 1947 Act has in most areas not even been thoroughly planned, let alone realized. Some of the reasons for this are administrative. The other reasons are that the Conservative Government, which has been in power during the crucial years, has no enthusiasm whatever for creative planning, and that there is still no 'public opinion' on planning. These two reasons are related in more ways than one. Much planning is at present conducted in secret. It has to be, or anticipation of the plans would enable speculators in property to make even larger fortunes than they do already. The people who are to be affected by the plans are not consulted about them before they are drawn up. The result is that when completed plans are finally disclosed, they often have to be withdrawn. If the Government had done something about land values, none of this would be necessary. Planning could be conducted openly, and indeed with deliberate publicity in order to develop public interest. In the long run, of course, public opinion on planning can best be created by examples of planning. To take a simple example, widespread indignation over the inadequacy of our roads can be dated from the opening of the first motor-way.

TOWN PLANNING

Worthing illustrates both the strength and weakness of post-war planning. It is a nicer place than it would have been if no planning powers had existed. The rows of bungalows and houses have been built of a height, along wide roads, and amenities and open spaces have been provided. Yet it can-not even be said that the negative function of planning has been fulfilled. Residential development along the coast from Southwick to Littlehampton has been so rapid that it is twelve years ahead of the county development plan (and the vastly increased elderly population has yet to be pro-vided with the extra hospital beds it needs). While there is still scope for redevelopment of old property, virgin space can be found only in the few remaining gaps between coastal towns and inland. Yet when the county planning officer put it to the Worthing Borough Council that they should slow down (not actually stop) their expansion, he was called a dictator and 'the King Canute of West Sussex' for his pains.

Each year there are 700-odd more deaths than births in Worthing. Yet its population (including visitors when the Census was taken) has risen from 69,431 in 1951 to 80,143 in 1961, or by more than a thousand a year. The number of homes rose over the same period from 22,753 to 29,100, or by 635 a year. And even these figures tell nothing like the whole story, for they take no account of the young people moving out of Worthing. A report on *Internal Migration* covering the two years from September 1948 to September 1950 revealed that 13,788 people moved out of Worthing and 15,907 moved in. Of those going out, 37 per cent were between twenty and forty years of age, and of those moving in 25 per cent were over sixty. The years covered by this report were not typical. None the less, one may safely say that if Worthing is to maintain its present rate of expansion, it must attract several thousand new residents a year. Since the Worthing Borough Council seems resolved to get the population up to the six figures regarded as a qualification for county-borough status, what space there is will no doubt be used.

In the actual manner of Worthing's expansion, what was arguably a unique planning opportunity has been lost. From an early date it was predictable that an unlimited number of retired people would want to live there. There was no problem, as with companies' demand for offices in London, of deciding how many could as well go somewhere else. People were moving to Worthing for the climate and the scenery, which could not be reproduced elsewhere. The planners' brief wrote itself – to arrange for the largest possible number of people to live in Worthing, without destroying its character. This implied keeping a lot of open space, building a good number of high blocks of flats, and putting up both blocks of flats and terraces of houses at arbitrary angles, with trees and slopes in between, so that the countryside would not appear to stop abruptly where the housing began.

The rapid expansion of Worthing's population can itself be vindicated, but not the manner in which it has been accommodated. After the early years of converting old houses into flats, there was a long period when new bungalows were erected in every direction. Belatedly, the local authority is now encouraging the building of flats, including high blocks. Thus the position of the blocks of flats has not been determined by any three-dimensional plan. In 1958 the local authority did approve a plan for the redevelopment of part of the central area. The local auctioneers and estate agents were sufficiently moved by this plan to engage a firm of planning consultants to produce a better one covering a wider area.

In February 1962 Mr R. B. Connell resigned, after eleven years as chief planning assistant of Worthing. He had proposed a master plan for the development of the whole of the town centre and the Victorian areas adjoining it. The chairmen of the development sub-committee and of the town planning committee both declared categorically that a master plan was not a practical possibility: it would place the dead hand of planning, the 'blight', upon the whole of the areas designated. The fact is that, with planning powers and no master plan, even private developers are at a loss. They have to prepare their own plans without knowing the conditions to be fulfilled and, when they have worked on them for months, may be arbitrarily refused planning permission. At the time of writing, Worthing is so far free from the dead hand of planning that nearly all sites cleared for redevelopment are being used as temporary car parks, and its main traffic routes are undecided.

Worthing is a district where planning has been treated seriously if unimaginatively. To find a truly offensive lack of planning, one has to go to smaller seaside resorts which, unlike Worthing, do not seek to attract large numbers of permanent residents. In places ranging from old Cornish fishing villages to the flat but pleasant coast of East Anglia, holiday homes have been erected higgledy-piggledy without pretence of individual design. Again the demand was predictable, and opportunities of starting virtually from scratch have been lost.

Elsewhere in the country, unless one is building a New Town, planning is of course bedevilled by what already exists. It is in the nature of things that the underdeveloped countries of the East and Africa, able to draw on European and American experience, should have finer cities to show

than any in this country. Chandigarh, the new capital of
the Punjab, has splendid architecture, and the pedestrians
and bullock-carts are rigidly separated. But from a planners'
point of view Britain is better off than many 'developed'
countries, in that it has a great deal of building that is so
old and dilapidated and generally undesirable that the case
for pulling it down is self-evident; and, cities having spread
slowly outwards, the building most in need of replacement is
in the centre.

Most towns now have their maps of proposed redevelopment, but they rarely amount to plans and are even more
rarely accompanied by three-dimensional models. Even the
full-scale plans may be so unprofessional as not to include
sufficient car parks or not to segregate pedestrians and traffic
in shopping centres. When such plans are submitted to the
Royal Fine Art Commission, they are returned with a cour-
teous suggestion that the local authority should employ a
consultant. It should of course be the Government's responsibility to see that planning consultants and traffic engineers
are employed on such plans from the outset. More important still, the Government should see that such plans are
produced quickly, and that no substantial redevelopment
occurs in city centres until they have been approved.

Since building licences were abolished in 1954, private
developers have been putting up office blocks in many cities
and towns besides London. Planning permission has to be
obtained for every one; but, unless the detailed plans submitted by developers have to conform to an outline plan for
a wide area, traffic problems can never be solved, there will
be no character deriving from the architecture as a whole,
and there may be no suitable sites retained for community
centres, libraries, and parks.

The greatest scope for planning is afforded by the New
Towns; and the Government's reluctance to create them,
being also responsible for the extent of the congestion in the

conurbations, is doubly to be deplored. Of the fifteen existing New Towns (in Britain), perhaps only the earliest and the latest, Stevenage and Cumbernauld, would get alphas if submitted as planning theses; but taken as a whole, and despite some fairly crude mistakes such as failure to provide garages, they are cause for satisfaction; compared with the non-new towns, they are a cause for pride. In New Towns as in everything else, lessons are learned from experience. Cumbernauld employs original planning concepts, and in the L.C.C.'s plan for a New Town at Hook in Hampshire (which was vetoed by the Hampshire County Council and given no support by the Government) these were carried farther. Instead of having scattered open spaces, Hook would have been so densely populated that the neighbouring countryside would have been within walking distance for everyone. To oversimplify slightly, the town centre would have been on stilts, safe for shoppers and children everywhere, with the traffic passing below. Hook might even have borne comparison with Chandigarh.

REGIONAL AND NATIONAL PLANNING

The need for regional planning being now generally accepted, we may expect to see some sort of regional bodies set up, even if they are only committees with representatives from various Ministries and the local authorities. When people say we need regional planning, they do not merely mean that we need planning over a wider area. What everyone wants is national planning. Regional authorities are to be the administrative means of achieving it. Regional authorities will need to cooperate among themselves, or be coordinated from the centre. In theory at least, regional planning could be achieved by cooperation between or coordination of the counties and county boroughs.

To a large extent, the failure of the existing planning

authorities to cooperate is attributable to conflicting interest and local prejudice, and this problem will not disappear with the appointment of regional authorities. To a large extent, however, it is also attributable to their smallness. Because of their smallness, they cannot afford the necessary specialists. Because of their smallness, there are too many of them either for effective cooperation or for effective coordination by the central Government. (If there were ten regional authorities, each would have under it only some fourteen or fifteen counties and county boroughs.) Lastly, because of their smallness, it is common for people to live under the jurisdiction of one planning authority but to work under the jurisdiction of another. Conurbations have spread across county borders, and the jurisdiction of individual counties is interrupted by county boroughs. Of the five million people in the geographical county of Lancashire, two million live within seventeen county boroughs. The boundaries of the new regions must be drawn so that it is exceptional for people to live in one and work in another.

Each regional authority would be responsible for drawing up a twenty-year development plan and for revising it every five years thereafter. This would say where and when New Towns were to be built, where and when existing towns were to be expanded, and where and when new roads were to be built or existing ones improved. It would broadly determine land use – notably, it would designate the green belts. Just as each regional plan would be drawn up in the context of a national plan, so the local authorities would have to draw up their own development plans within the context of the regional plan; and in turn the actual developers, whether public or private, would have to draw up their site plans in the context of a local development plan. The regional authority would be responsible for there being three-dimensional models of the new city centres and of other extensive redevelopment. One could then expect that city centres would incorporate at least the obvious town-planning principles, such as the reservation of a substantial area to pedestrians and the provision of adequate car parks. Motorists should of course be made to pay an economic rent for the land they use when they park their cars (as distinct from being forbidden to park them anywhere near where they want to go or else forbidden to park them for as long as they want). Valuations made for the purpose of a land tax would help in the calculation of appropriate parking fees. In the very congested cities they would be high enough to deter many motorists from going to work in their cars. Money for the improvement of public-transport services would come both from the high parking fees and from the increase in the number of passengers. (One of the rare hurtful suggestions made in *Change and Challenge* for solving the problem of the London region is that train fares should be raised.)

We saw earlier that the population in the 20–35-mile belt round the London conurbation could, on present trends, increase from 4·3 million to 6·5 million over the next twenty years. Of this prospective increase of 2·2 million, about a quarter of a million is accounted for by people who will move in from outside the London region altogether. The London region, with 27 per cent of Britain's population, gained nearly 40 per cent of the new jobs created in Britain between 1952 and 1960. In 1959–60 the London region gained about 40,000 insured employees (most of them young, and all set to get married and start having children) from Scotland, the north of England, and Wales. Thus the problem is twofold. There is the process occurring in and around the conurbations – Birmingham, Merseyside, Manchester, and Bristol as well as London – whereby more and more people work at the centre and live ever farther out. There is the further tendency for people to be drawn towards the conurbations from elsewhere, and in particular to be drawn to the London region. Both these problems will be greatly mitigated if we introduce a land tax (or the ground rents proposed by *Socialist Commentary*). A land tax will reduce the demand for land for offices and industry. Small industry, which escapes the control of the Industrial Development Certificates (required to build or extend premises in excess of 5,000 square feet), would be very responsive to a tax. With fewer jobs in the congested areas, fewer people will be drawn to them. With a high land tax on houses in the congested areas, more retired people would move out of them. (People working would be less affected since salaries and wages – or bonuses – must always be related to the local cost of housing.)

The problem of the concentration of commerce in the centres must be solved by building more New Towns and expanding existing towns outside the conurbations. To some extent this merely means moving the jobs out to where people are already living. It also of course means moving population – 'overspill'. The capital for each of the New Towns has been advanced from public funds and vested in a development corporation. Under the New Towns Act, 1959, it was provided that as each New Town was substantially completed, the development corporation should be dissolved and its assets and liabilities handed over to the Commission for New Towns. Apart from the New Towns, housing for 'overspill' population has been financed, with the aid of Exchequer subsidies, either by the 'exporting' authority, or (under the Town Development Act, 1952) by the receiving authority (or by both authorities). The proposed regional authorities would be able to finance housing for 'overspill' wherever it thought it appropriate to do so. Until recently the Government neglected the problem of 'overspill'. Since the Conservatives came to power, no New Town has been begun in England and Wales (and only one, Cumbernauld, in Scotland). Since its recognition that green belts do not of themselves constitute planning, the Government has increased the subsidy for 'overspill' housing (in the 1961 Housing Act), has designated the sixteenth New Town at Skelmersdale outside Liverpool, and has promised more – which is to say that we are doing in 1962 rather less than we should have done in 1952.

The drift to the south-east must be stopped or reduced, by developing a number of cities or towns in other parts of the country to the point where they have the essential attractions of the cities on which the conurbations are based. Each region should develop its own centre with large-scale commercial, medical, educational, and cultural services. Generally speaking, people will go to live where jobs and amenities are available. How does one persuade firms to establish factories and offices where they are wanted? The present policy is to attract them to depressed areas by offering them financial inducements – by paying them to go where they do not want to go. This may always be necessary in some degree, but it is not planning. Firms go where industrial and commercial amenities are available. The community should therefore provide them where it wants firms to go. This fundamental principle of national planning, drawn to the Government's attention in *Change and Challenge*, has been illustrated by Caerphilly in Glamorganshire, with its population of 37,000. The local authority spent £30,000 on a 17-acre industrial estate, where all essential services were provided. Firms quickly applied for sites, and it was decided to build a second estate. Caerphilly has solved its unemployment problem itself. This is the principle to apply, both in reviving depressed areas and in developing regional centres. It is an example of how to contrive things so that choices made by individuals are compatible with the interests of the community. It is not axiomatic that all the depressed areas ought to be revived, but in general it is the simplest planning solution. In some of the depressed areas, we should already have had a problem of surplus houses but for the increase in the number of households.

Of all the services required by industry, the most important is provision for transport. There are already nine million motor vehicles in Britain, and thirteen million are expected by the end of the 1960s. The Government has acknowledged the urgency of the problem with a greatly expanded road-building programme, which it likes to think of as planning. It is an attempt to make up for a lack of planning, and a forlorn one. In national planning as in house building, there is need for a great deal more research, but we can learn from America's crudest mistakes even without research. The nine million vehicles now on our roads are all going to Birmingham. By building motorways to Birmingham, we are ensuring that the thirteen million on our roads at the end of the 1960s will all be going there too. Birmingham's planning problems will have been multiplied by a factor of $\frac{13}{9}$. It would be better to build motorways to nowhere. If we stopped a motorway in the middle of a field, a factory would appear at the end of it in no time at all, and the company building it would happily build houses for its employees to live in. The first use of motorways should be to revive depressed areas and develop regional centres.

House building, the location of industry, and road building are now determined by separate and even contradictory ministerial policies. *Socialist Commentary* proposes that a new Ministry of Town and Country Planning should be created, with far greater responsibilities than the former one or the present Ministry of Housing and Local Government.

It would have supreme control in planning the location of employment, of housing and communications, coordinating the specific plans of the Ministry of Housing and Local Government, the Ministry of Education, the Board of Trade and the Ministry of Transport.

This is probably the only way to achieve both a unified and a satisfactory planning policy. The new Ministry of Town and Country Planning would stand to the Ministry of Housing and Local Government, the Ministry of Education, and the Board of Trade roughly as the Ministry of Defence stands to the Service Ministries. In planning matters, the regional authorities should be directly responsible to it.

10 Policy and Politics

WE have been feeling our way towards a national policy for housing. We have seen how regional authorities could get houses erected in the right places. Since we want to build many more houses and associated amenities than at present, we must consider where, apart from increased efficiency, the money is to come from. The difficulty is not in writing the cheques, but in preventing inflation. We have to stop spending on other purposes to the extent of the extra money we are going to spend on housing. Where, in this sense, is the money coming from? Schedule A on owner-occupied houses could bring in £200 million for a start. A land tax would bring in an ever-increasing amount. More could be got by devoting to housing a greater proportion of the proceeds of general taxation and of the capital raised by public borrowing. The rest we must get in one or more ways from the consumers – the householders themselves. Their subsidies could be withdrawn. Their controlled rents could be raised. Their mortgage interest could be increased – enabling the interest paid on capital borrowed from the public to be increased and hence more to be borrowed. They could be given financial incentives to spend more on current housing, or to save more for future housing.

We also have to consider whom the State is going to assist with the cost of housing. A council tenant should not have his rent subsidized in one district but not in another. An owner-occupier should not be able to get a 100 per cent mortgage from a local authority in one district but not in another. Nor should a would-be owner-occupier in a district where all the houses are old be unable to get a mortgage at all. Even more serious than the regional anomalies are the class anomalies. The State gives no financial aid whatever to private tenants, many of whom could not even afford the rent of a subsidized council house. It gives the greatest aid to rich owner-occupiers. If we say that we now treat housing as a social service, we mock the poor.

The obvious qualifications for help with housing are being poor and having a lot of dependants. In the place of subsidized rents, rent control, and the abolition of Schedule A, the State should give allowances, tied to expenditure on housing, according to a scale that decreases with higher income and increases with the number of dependents. In substituting national allowances for subsidies, we should relieve the local authorities as landlords of their obligation to assess their tenants' ability to pay. In substituting them for rent control, we should remove the relative injustice suffered by tenants of non-controlled dwellings, and make it possible for private enterprise to build new low-cost housing for rent. This in turn would make possible widespread urban renewal.

We also wish to encourage people to spend more of their own resources on housing. Our scale of allowances should therefore increase with the proportion of income that the householder is devoting to housing. The minimum proportion for qualification for this additional allowance might be a fifth. It is true that under such a scheme a man spending a higher proportion of his income on housing could increase his allowance from the State by reducing his income – by doing less overtime. He could qualify for an increased allowance on two scores: that his income had decreased; and that the proportion of his income spent on housing had increased. But this does not make the scheme open to as much objection as the present differential rents. In order to increase his housing allowance in this way, a man would have to forgo a significant amount of income. A man spending a high proportion of his income on housing would be more reluctant than most to do this.

Every householder earning below a certain income should have his own housing account with the State. Everything he paid into his account should be increased by the appropriate allowance, whether it was spent on current housing or saved. Housing expenses payable out of the account would include rent, rates, mortgage repayments and interest, ground rent, repairs, decorations, legal fees, estate agents' fees, the costs of moving (up to a certain amount), and of course the payment of part of the purchase price of a house in order to reduce the amount of the mortgage and the subsequent cost in mortgage interest. So that householders should not be discouraged from saving in this way, provision should be made for them to withdraw their savings, less accumulated allowances, for any purpose whatever. All savings would of course accumulate interest.

To avoid inequity between owner-occupiers and tenants, we must treat a certain capital value for each householder as a social service. Initially the value might be £3,000. (It could be made rather higher in districts where the price of land or the land tax is high, but for the most part it should be left to employers who want offices or factories in these districts to pay salaries and wages that cover the higher cost of housing.) The council tenant and the private tenant will be entitled all their adult lives to housing allowances to help with the rents of houses of up to £3,000 in value, or, for example, to help with three-quarters of the rent of a house valued at £4,000. The owner-occupier will be able to get a 100 per cent mortgage on a house of up to £3,000, or to buy a more expensive house and have the first £3,000 treated on social-service terms and the excess on the traditional building-society terms. Once he has acquired £3,000-worth of house on social-service terms, he will not be entitled to any more housing allowances for mortgage payments, unless he has to sell his house at a loss. (He will still be entitled to use savings in his housing account for expenses such as repairs and the costs of moving.) If, however, he has bought a £3,000 house and has only had a £2,500 mortgage on it, then, when the mortgage is repaid, he is still owed £500-worth of housing on social-service terms. In principle he might be given a sum on completion of the repayment of the mortgage, to compensate him for the extra housing allowances he would have received with a 100 per cent mortgage. But we are allowing the potential owner-occupier's savings towards a down payment to qualify for a contribution in housing allowances, and when there are available both 100 per cent mortgages and housing allowances to assist with mortgage interest, we want to provide the greatest incentive to make a large down payment. A down payment paid from savings other than those in a housing account should therefore qualify for a capital payment equivalent (with a deduction for interest) to the extra housing allowances that would be granted over the ensuing years with a 100 per cent mortgage. This is to say that a man will deposit a certain sum as a down payment and it will count as a larger sum.

The prospective housing allowances in respect of which the increase is granted will have to be calculated on the man's current income, whereas his income over the ensuing years may rise even to the point where he does not qualify for allowances. This is certainly an incentive to make as large a down payment as possible. We shall be favouring those with low incomes and a little capital; but this cannot be avoided, if we are to let weekly savings towards a deposit qualify for contributions from housing allowances, because the man with capital could pay a small amount into his housing account each week. We have to be prepared to carry the principle to its logical conclusion. Suppose that a man earning £10 a week inherits a £3,000 house. He will be assessed under Schedule A for the income this house represents to him, but, even if Schedule A were based on current values, his income would still be only about £13 a week. He will have a claim on the State in respect of the housing allowances he is never going to draw. Where it meets a large claim, the State can of course reserve the right to recover all or part of it, if over the next twenty years, say, the man's income rises.

We are in any case favouring the owner-occupier by allowing him to concentrate the cost of a lifetime's housing into twenty or thirty years and so to qualify for higher allowances. The marginal case makes this clear. Consider a tenant of a house worth say £3,000 who pays a rent (including rates) which is a fraction less than a fifth of his income. If he remains a tenant all his life, he will never receive a housing allowance (except as an old-age pensioner). If he buys a £3,000 house (when his mortgage repayments plus interest will be greater than his rent), he will begin to receive allowances. The rest of the community will, however, have struck a fair bargain with him. The owner-occupier's additional expenditure on housing in the short term is saving – is money withdrawn from circulation which enables the community as a whole to build extra houses without inflation.

Our scheme must provide for a man who has paid for all or most of his house and sells it without buying another one. He is unlikely to do this merely to raise money, since he can take out another mortage. But he may do it if he is going abroad; or if he is moving to another part of the country where the house he most likes is rented, or where he is not proposing to stay long. If he has bought his house with the aid of housing allowances, the State will recover from the proceeds of the sale a sum to take account of the difference (plus interest) between the housing allowances he has received and the lower ones (if any) he could have received over the years towards rent. Thereafter he will be entitled to housing allowances to assist with rent. Alternatively, if he intends to buy another house in the future, and wishes to claim housing allowances to assist with its purchase, he can ask for all the allowances he has received in the past to be deducted from the price at which he sells his house.

When a council or private tenant dies, his housing allowances will die with him. If the same is to be true of an owner-occupier, an amount must be payable from his estate equal to that which the State would have claimed if, while still alive, he had sold the house without buying another. If, however, the house is inherited by his widow and remains in her possession, then the allowances need not be repaid until her death. The widows of tenants will be eligible for housing allowances. If repayment were claimed from the estate of an owner-occupier when he had a widow, she would become eligible for housing allowances in her own right. Anyone other than a widow who inherits a house and lives in it will be able to get a mortgage for the amount of the repayment. If he is entitled to housing allowances, he will receive them towards the cost of the mortgage payments – and as we have seen, he will also be able to claim them in respect of the remaining capital value of the house, up to £3,000.

The council tenant or private tenant who has been drawing housing allowances to help with rent, and then decides to become an owner-occupier, will have to accept a deduction from his future allowances for repayment of past ones. This will not arise often. The man aspiring to become an owner-occupier will not wish to claim housing allowances in respect of rent. He will prefer to reserve all he is entitled to for the purchase of his own house, and to save money in his housing account knowing that it is being increased by the State.

If we are to give 100 per cent mortgages freely, we must

know what we are going to do when an owner-occupier needs to move and can sell his house only at a loss. Let us take the extreme case. As Michael Shanks points out in *The Stagnant Society*, in the anthracite coal-mining areas of south-west Wales, now in decline, an unusually large number of workers own their own houses:

These people face a cruel dilemma. If they are to move elsewhere in search of work, even assuming they can find accommodation, they will have to sell their own houses – and in a declining community it will clearly be hard to find buyers. There is thus the choice of a serious capital loss or unemployment. All the Ministry can do in such cases at present is to help pay solicitors' and house agents' costs, up to a maximum of £50, if the worker wants to sell his old house or buy a new one.*

It is clear that many men in this dilemma will choose unemployment – and unemployment benefit and National Assistance. If the prospective capital loss is greater than the original deposit plus the amount of mortgage repaid, a man can scarcely do other than choose unemployment. Clearly it is in the State's own interest to help men in this predicament, whether by itself buying up the house, as Michael Shanks proposes, or simply by meeting a share of the loss on the sale to a private buyer. The negative operation of a land tax would reduce losses on houses, but further provision is necessary, not only to encourage mobility of labour and keep down the cost of supporting the unemployed, but to satisfy the demands of equity. One cannot encourage people earning average wages to spend every penny they can afford on becoming property-owning democrats, and then sting them for a £500 capital loss. Up to a certain amount (an amount related to his income) the owner should bear the loss himself. Beyond that point the State should share in it, and the greater the loss (again in proportion to income)

* Penguin Books, 1961.

the greater the State's share should be. For the amount of
the loss he himself has to bear, the owner should be able to
go into debt on his housing account with the State.

It is conceivable that a man selling his house might come
to an arrangement with the purchaser whereby the true
price was not declared, and he shared with him what he
received from the State for his supposed loss. But the declared price would have to be significantly below the true
price for such an arrangement to be profitable, and house
prices in any one area are known. Wherever suspicion was
incurred, the State itself would buy the house at the declared price – the mere possibility of which should be
enough to deter anyone from trying to cheat.

By whom is the State to be represented in all these trans-
actions? They call for the experience of both the Inland
Revenue and the building societies. We have seen that
public funds provided for mortgages can be successfully
distributed through the building societies as at present con-
stituted. The building societies handled the £100,000 that
the Government made available for the purchase of old
houses between 1959 and 1961. None the less, it would be
tidier if the large building societies (or their housing depart-
ments) were nationalized and Inland Revenue officials
added to their staffs. Any building societies too small to be
made use of economically would have to be compensated
for their loss of business. We have seen that nationalization
of the building societies would be a peculiarly painless
operation, and there are advantages in nationalization besides administrative convenience.

Once nationalized, the building societies could be told
not to discriminate against old houses and houses that
looked like council houses. They would be told in fact to
grant a mortgage on any house, subject only to a surveyor's
report. In granting mortgages on old houses, they would
have discretion to increase their normal interest rate. Where

a surveyor's report indicated that a house needed and justi-fied repairs or the installation of amenities, then the mort-gage would cover the cost (less any improvement grant), and the expenditure would be obligatory on the owner. If aesthetic prejudice manifested itself, it would be in the valuation of new houses, and particularly of the more ex-pensive ones. The building societies would be required to give the same percentage mortgage on all houses over £3,000 (at their own valuations). Provision could be made that whenever the valuation was significantly below the average valuation of houses of the same cubic content in the same area, it should automatically be referred to the plan-ning authorities; and that a prospective mortgagor should have the right, for a fee, to appeal to the planning authori-ties against any valuation. This provision would apply equally to valuations of rented houses. There is, however, no reason to assume that prejudice against modern design would persist once the building societies were nationalized. The present excess of the demand for mortgages over the funds available makes possible extreme financial caution. The policy is not inspired by reactionary tastes, or the build-ing societies would be readier to finance the purchase of old houses. It is entirely uninfluenced by aesthetic considera-tions.

We now have to do a rather complicated account to see where the money for our increased building programme is coming from. Introducing 100 per cent mortgages will be inflationary. Because we shall charge higher mortgage inter-est rates (allowing repayment over a longer period) we shall be free to pay higher interest for money we borrow and hence shall be able to borrow more, which will be disinflationary. The housing allowances themselves will be inflationary. Against them we may set the abolition of subsidies, the decontrol of private rented dwellings, and £200 million a year in Schedule A. The extra proportion of their incomes that people will spend on housing – even perhaps the higher incomes they will set out to earn in order to have more to spend on housing – will be disinflationary. So will the encouragement to saving. To provide mortgages on old houses on which they cannot now be obtained will be inflationary. Against this we can set the preservation of these houses from decay, and a consequent reduction in the building necessary over the next twenty to forty years. Lastly we have the pure disinflationary gain of an original land tax.

With the housing allowances based on the proportion of their incomes which people spend on housing at present, and with higher mortgage interest rates to be fixed at the State's discretion, we can be confident of contriving things so that the disinflationary forces exceed the inflationary. We must recognize, however, that the various means of paying for our building programme bear no direct relation to the expenditure on it. National income and expenditure similarly bear no direct relation to each other, and, just as the Chancellor of the Exchequer has to adjust interest rates and taxes in order to balance them, so we must be prepared to adjust mortgage interest rates and even the housing allowances themselves, in order to balance the national housing income and the national housing expenditure.

In order, then, to treat housing as a social service on a national footing, we need to abolish subsidized rents; abolish rent control; restore Schedule A to its full value; introduce a complicated new system of housing allowances; impose regional authorities on the local authorities; deprofessionalize the architects; professionalize the estate agents; and nationalize the building societies. Can it be done? Is it worth the fuss?

HOUSING IN PERSPECTIVE

In the forties we defeated Hitler and laid the foundations of
the Welfare State. In the fifties we drew with Nasser and
passed the Rent Act. There is evidence that the sixties could
be another decade of endeavour; but there is a danger that
the politicians will not recognize it. Politicians have their
ears so close to the ground that they somehow get below
hearing distance of the social conscience. Labour, it must
be remembered, was confident it would lose the 1945
Election. They were good men in the post-war Labour
Government, but were they so brave that they really intended
to nationalize the Bank of England, the railways, the min-
ers, and the doctors, and free India, all at one swoop?
Although the Labour Party today has a pretty broken look
about it, it does not discount the possibility of winning the
next election by default. There is therefore a real possibility
that it will find itself in power, restricted to a programme
adapted to the supposed moral mediocrity of the upper-
working-class floating voter. Next time, of course, it will
know whether or not it is going to win: the public-opinion
polls will tell it. Unfortunately the polls are not yet so
refined that they tell a party what is expected of it.

Political apathy and I'm-all-right-Jackism undoubtedly
exist. Must we not accept that they are the result of giving
people security – of introducing the Welfare State and
establishing full employment? We have not in fact given
people security. We have given them better education,
better medical services, and the assurance that they will
not starve when they are old or unemployed. We have given
them higher wages. But we have left them liable to be
evicted from their homes at a month's notice and to lose
their jobs at an hour's notice. What we have created is
prosperity without security, a condition which always has
been and always will be associated with political apathy

and I'm-all-right-Jackism. These are the attributes of white mercenaries in the Congo and of business men making money quickly in a line that will not last. They are not notable among the secure middle classes, whether they are managing directors or clerks.

The post-war myth is that we live in a Welfare State where each individual has his economic needs satisfied regardless of his deserts and is scarcely given the opportunity of taking any initiative for himself. The reality is different. The head of a family evicted from its home at a week's notice may be a competent and industrious workman not lacking in enterprise. After a full day's work and overtime he may spend hours every evening searching for a flat or rooms he can afford. Weeks later he may still be homeless and separated from his family. Just walk up to him one day and explain to him that he is coddled.

Even if he lives in a council house or owns his own house, he still has to reckon with redundancy – with finding himself suddenly out of work with negligible compensation or even none at all. It is small solace that because there is full employment he should find another job within a few weeks. For the pre-war worker who was poor even when he was working, the pittance provided by the State, though it did not prevent suffering, at least prevented financial disaster. For today's worker who is buying his own house, or who is buying furniture and consumer goods on hire-purchase – and who cannot cut down his commitments as he can his smoking, drinking, and eating – unemployment benefits, even supplemented by National Assistance, may not be enough to stave off financial disaster.

The difficulties are multiplied when finding a new job means moving. The pre-war worker paying a rent of a few shillings a week could find similar accommodation more or less anywhere, and the cost of moving his chattels, while significant, was not prohibitive. Today's worker is a good deal less mobile. If he is buying his own house, it will be expensive to sell it and buy another one. If he is living in a council house and has to give it up, he will not get another one in a new area: his name will go on the bottom of a waiting list. And anywhere where there is work to move to, there is likely to be a housing shortage – itself partly the result of increased prosperity.

There has been an even bigger change. No shame attached to the mass unemployment of the pre-war years. Those experiencing it felt bitterness, but they felt also a *camaraderie*, a sense of righteousness, and a pride in their own stoicism. It is a different matter, in the present materialist and status-conscious age, for a man to find that, alone among his neighbours, he cannot afford to keep his television set. To have substituted short-term redundancy for long-term unemployment is social progress. None the less, because long-term unemployment invoked the feelings appropriate to a natural disaster, whereas short-term redundancy invokes feelings more appropriate to bankruptcy, the fact is that in the post-war years we have vastly increased the worker's psychological insecurity.

The post-war myth was largely of the working-class's own making. Under the Labour Government it experienced a nambypamby mood, a readiness to rely for the future on working-class solidarity and the soaking of the rich. That mood is spent. The prosperous worker knows that the amount of his own income tax can be a significant determinant of his standard of living. He knows that prosperity brings new problems of insecurity, and recognizes intuitively that everyone will have to share in the cost of their solution. He has discovered that he never believed in egalitarianism proper, and believes in it even less amid prosperity. He will go on strike in defence of a differential. He does not question the differentials between skilled workers and managing directors. He is even beginning to feel an identity of interest with the professional manager as against the large share-holder (he may be a small shareholder himself), the stock-broker, and the property-developer. That he has rejected equality does not mean he no longer has a social conscience. For equality he has substituted equity.

When the *People* says much the same as *The Economist*, it is time for the politicians to take note. (*The Times* and the *Mirror* were saying much the same in 1945.) And in an article in the *People** entitled 'Our Charter for the homeless in 1962' the main points were:

THROW OUT ALL THE RICH COUNCIL TENANTS NOW
BRING IN DIFFERENTIAL RENT SCHEMES NOW
MAKE SURE ALL COUNCIL HOUSES ARE FULLY OCCUPIED

The article said:

The third point in our charter – the problem of under-occu-pied houses – needs men with hearts of steel to insist upon it. But it must be done. Many of these houses are occupied by widows, or by middle-aged couples whose families have left home and married. Understandably, many are reluctant to leave.

We respect their feelings. But we still say they must go. . . .
To solve the housing problem we will have to be ruthless.

Ruthlessness, not nambypambyness, is now fashionable, but fashionable only if it is employed in support of equity. Ruthlessness in ignoring the problem of the homeless may of itself lose the Conservatives the next election. A readiness to be ruthless in solving it might ensure that Labour won it other than by default.

It is generally recognized that the one idea with which the Labour Party has secured a spontaneous response from the electorate since 1951 was its pension scheme. This provided ultimately for everyone to draw a retirement pen-

* 31 December 1961.

sion equal to half his earnings. It was thus concerned with the two factors we have been discussing, security and equity, distinguishing equity from equality – or with security in the standard of living to which one has become accustomed. Labour has not drawn the moral. In 1961 it made the important decision that its next election manifesto would propose legislation to compel the payment of compensation for redundancy, but it has said so little about it since that it must be unaware of its importance.

Worst of all, the Labour Party still presents itself as striving to achieve, in Douglas Jay's phrase, the minimum practicable inequality. Could anything be more depressing, more insulting, more patronizing? People are told that re-grettably they are acquisitive and slothful. If they were fit to be human, they would all want to live in a house exactly the same size as everyone else, and receive the same earnings as everyone else, while competing with others only for the right to work longer hours for the greater good of society. Fear not, however; for the Labour Party will indulge their weakness just sufficiently to keep the wheels of production turning. The lack of moral content in contemporary Con-servative philosophy undoubtedly sickens people, but it must count for a lot that the Conservatives do not tell them their every aspiration is vile. Why not a property-owning democracy and the Devil take the hindmost, if the only alternative is to feel guilty at owning a bigger toothbrush than your neighbour?

I have been arguing that the Labour Party could win the next election on the related issues of housing and redundancy. Hypothetically, the Conservative Party could win it on the same issues. It came to power in 1951 on a promise that it would build 300,000 houses a year, and it kept the promise. There is nothing that needs to be done now that is alien to the true Conservative tradition, which has more in it of paternalism than of *laissez-faire*. But so long as they ignore homelessness, toy with the slums, reject planning, and let house prices soar, the Conservatives should not be difficult to beat.

To keep things in perspective, I am not arguing that the result of the next election ought to be determined by housing. Better by far that people should vote on disarmament, Berlin, the Common Market, and Central African Federation, or that, if they must concentrate on domestic issues, they should give priority over housing to the structure of industry – to finding some better distribution of power, wealth, and responsibility than is afforded either by the existing nationalized industries or the existing private companies. The point is that those who do vote strictly according to conscience are for the most part middle-class intellectuals who are well housed and reasonably secure in their incomes. Let us give the nation security, then see how it behaves.